# My Gateway to Heaven

Linda Virage

Copyright © 2022 by Linda Virage

All rights reserved. No part of this book may be reproduced or transmitted in any form or by any means, electronic or mechanical, including photocopying, recording or by any information storage and retrieval system without permission in writing from the author.

Book artwork: Illustrations Hub

www.illustrationshub.com

ISBN: 978-0-6454960-0-0

Published by: Linda Virage

# Dedication

To all Christians and non-Christians worldwide who are seeking the truth and the true purpose of life.

# Contents

| | |
|---|---|
| PREFACE | I |
| INTRODUCTION | 1 |
| CHAPTER 1 | 15 |
| CHAPTER 2 | 25 |
| CHAPTER 3 | 32 |
| CHAPTER 4 | 39 |
| CHAPTER 5 | 45 |
| CHAPTER 6 | 51 |
| CHAPTER 7 | 59 |
| CHAPTER 8 | 65 |
| CHAPTER 9 | 73 |
| CHAPTER 10 | 79 |
| CHAPTER 11 | 86 |
| CHAPTER 12 | 94 |
| CHAPTER 13 | 104 |
| CHAPTER 14 | 112 |
| CHAPTER 15 | 120 |
| CHAPTER 16 | 128 |
| CHAPTER 17 | 135 |
| CHAPTER 18 | 145 |
| CHAPTER 19 | 154 |
| CHAPTER 20 | 166 |
| CHAPTER 21 | 172 |
| CHAPTER 22 | 185 |
| CHAPTER 23 | 193 |
| CHAPTER 24 | 205 |
| CHAPTER 25 | 217 |
| CHAPTER 26 | 223 |
| CHAPTER 27 | 235 |

# PREFACE

I know that there are people out there in this world who are much worse off than I am, and I'd like to acknowledge that I'm not in any way, shape or form, trying to detract from this fact. But I also know that there are people out there who are in a similar situation to myself and who may benefit from reading about my life experiences including my countless visions, religious dreams as well as my many supernatural occurrences which prove that God is real and that we should continually set our sights on going to Heaven as our final destination and build on the Grace that Jesus has so generously bestowed upon us through Baptism.

For such a long period of time, I was afraid to take up my Cross and follow Jesus due to my continual and irrational fears in relation to the suffering that I believed being a Disciple of Jesus may bring. But my many irrational fears were both unsubstantiated and unjustified. And after having developed the necessary fortitude required, through the intercession of St Michael Archangel, I have proudly become a Disciple of Christ; I have taken up my Cross to follow Jesus and I now live my life in accordance with the Way, the Truth and the Life. And as a direct consequence of this, I have finally been able to experience true happiness in life.

During my life, however, I've been forced to climb mountains in the form of great obstacles that were, suddenly and most unexpectedly, thrown in my path, some of which seemed insurmountable to me, at first. But the key factor in all of my triumphs and successes in life is that I never allowed myself the luxury of giving up, and I continually turned to God for help in my time of need because I always knew that when man and/or doctors were unable to help me, God always could.

It's so easy to just give up when the going gets tough, but I never took the easy option. Although most challenging at times, I chose to take the difficult path since I knew that if I persisted, this path would at least have the potential to lead me to victory and beyond. I always fought back to the very best of my abilities, no matter what the circumstances were at the time.

And so, putting pen to paper, I came to the sudden realization, one day, when I was feeling particularly dejected and despondent, that in order to try to make any real sense of my life, it was imperative that I write a book about my life experiences, to help me gain some sort of perspective, clarity and understanding as to why my life has contained so much suffering, and why my life is in such a 'mess', even to this day, and at this particular point in time.

Much of my life has involved travelling through dark tunnels and although I eventually reached the light at the other side, I still feel as though I need to work out why my life has turned out the way it has in order to be able to turn over a new leaf, successfully leave my past behind, and be able to focus more on making the present and future as bright as they can possibly be.

If I'm able to inspire even one of my readers, through writing this book, who is embarking on their own personal and most difficult life journey, then I will have achieved my aim. And in my eyes, it will have been worth my while to muster up the courage to reflect on my past and simultaneously, to dredge up so many painful memories in an attempt to help others who may find themselves in a similar situation to mine in life.

It's important to note here that I have, without a doubt, also experienced great joy in my life for which I am extremely grateful.

But through my sorrows, I have learnt never to take anything in life for granted, and that life itself is a most precious commodity. We should always try our utmost to enjoy and appreciate each and every day because we really don't know what tomorrow may bring.

Although life may seem like it's just one continuous and arduous journey until we reach our individual and final destinations, we should never lose sight of the fact that we are constantly growing, acquiring new knowledge and maturing as a result of our own unique and different life experiences. For some of us, our life journey may contain an element of adventure, excitement, success and great happiness. But for others, our life journey may contain much suffering, melancholy, great despair, failure and only a certain degree of happiness in between. My life journey could be categorized as being the latter.

But I am beginning to realize that regardless of whether your life journey has taken on the former or the latter route, life is definitely something that should always be treasured, cherished and appreciated.

If we always try our utmost to retain our faith, trust and hope in God, as I have managed to do so throughout my life, in any given situation, and if we endeavour to seek help rather than suffer in silence, whenever we may be feeling isolated and trapped in our current lives, then anything is possible.

# INTRODUCTION

A terrifying and yet extraordinarily special event, a once in a lifetime experience, occurred in my life over eight years ago now which will be etched in my memory forever. This most significant event took place on a Friday night, only two days before Mother's Day. And on this particular night, the Blessed Virgin Mary, the Mother of God, appeared to me in a personal Apparition in a dream which shook me to my core - a dream which was a prophecy that would become reality a number of years later, unbeknown to me at the time.

Whilst still fast asleep in bed, I distinctly remember, first and foremost, hearing this most unusual and peculiar sound that I find extremely difficult to describe in words or even replicate verbally, for that matter.

And then, immediately afterwards, I remember feeling as though I was suddenly being transported to a different place that I didn't fully recognize. And then my dream began.

This most unusual and peculiar sound was a noise that I had definitely not heard before in the exact format that it was portrayed to me in my dream anyway, and hearing this sound did not frighten me. And I guess this sound could be likened to the sound of a clap of thunder, although extremely distorted since I failed to recognize the origins of this sound initially in my dream.

But in a way, I now feel that this most unusual noise had alerted my conscience whilst deeply asleep, and although I somehow knew that something was about to occur, I had no idea as to what this may be, and so I simply waited for some unknown event to begin to unfold.

I distinctly remember standing at the top of a staircase, and I knew that there was a building close by but my vision of the surrounding area was obscured and limited to only being able to see straight ahead; I could not see what was above or below me at the time. The nearby building that I could only partially see in view was light brown in colour, and I had an inkling that I was somewhere in the city but I was unsure of my exact location.

It's of the utmost importance to note here, however, that my sibling was also in my dream. I could always feel my sibling's presence and I knew, without a doubt, that she was standing next to me at the very beginning of my dream, even though I failed to be able to see her, in a visual sense.

And as my dream slowly began to unfold, I suddenly heard a loud booming male voice which appeared to be coming from high above me, from the sky. Somehow, I just knew that it was coming from Heaven, and the voice clearly said, "Hail Mary is going to hospital."

I remember thinking to myself, "Why would Hail Mary be going to hospital? She doesn't get sick." (At the time of my dream, I had referred to Our Lady as Hail Mary, and I had always addressed Her by this name whilst praying to the Mother of God in the past).

But nevertheless, I felt extremely excited at being given the opportunity to experience a potential sighting of Our Lady. And since I really wished to see Her in person, I waited patiently for Our Lady's arrival, but only to be bitterly disappointed from the onset.

A short moment later, I saw a carriage approach. It was an open carriage with very large wooden wheels attached to its wooden frame. It resembled a carriage from the olden days, and definitely differed in appearance to the modern-day carriages that exist today.

And inside this carriage, sat a Lady. She wore a very pale, baby blue coloured veil on Her head, and She had quite noticeably small blue eyes. I immediately observed that this Lady also had a number of wrinkles around Her eyes which had the effect of causing Her eyes to appear quite small in size.

I remember thinking to myself, in my dream, that this Lady could not actually be Hail Mary since She appeared to look rather old at the time. And because I had always imagined Our Lady to look young, I said to myself, "She must be a cute old Nun instead."

Shortly afterwards, however, the carriage came to a halt, and stopped right in front of where I was standing. This mysterious Lady stepped out of the carriage, and walked towards a white counter that was in the shape of a semicircle.

I walked over to this Lady and stood diagonally opposite Her, on the other side of the counter. I just stared at this Lady in wonder, but She failed to meet my gaze. I kept hoping that this Lady would eventually turn to face me, but She only continued to stare straight ahead and never directly at me, appearing to look quite expressionless at the time.

All of a sudden, my sibling, who was standing only a short distance away, called out to me. She said, "Linda, come over here. Look up at the sky. It's so beautiful!" And in spite of the fact that, in my heart and soul, I knew that I didn't want to leave the presence of this mysterious Lady, I reluctantly walked away from Her, and headed towards my sibling.

And looking up, I saw endless white clouds amidst a vast blue sky. The sky was filled with nothing but clouds. But the clouds didn't appear to look real to me; they were not beautiful white fluffy clouds that I had often seen in the past in the sky before.

In my view, these particular clouds looked as though they were fake in appearance. It's difficult to actually describe their true physical appearance in words, but I will now proceed to give you an analogy which I hope that you will be able to visualize and understand.

If you can imagine drawing short wavy lines or squiggles to represent water and waves in the ocean in an illustration or diagram, the clouds that I saw in my dream consisted of an infinite number of wavy lines amidst a vast blue sky, but these lines were actually white in colour rather than blue.

But what had really astonished me the most, at the time, was that my sibling had thought that these fake clouds were so beautiful. Personally, I had, in fact, been quite disappointed after having reluctantly walked over to my sibling in order to look up at the sky, only to see an infinite number of fake looking clouds being scattered everywhere, especially since I had not wished to leave this Lady's side in the first place. I had so desperately wanted to stay with Her in the hope that She would meet my gaze at long last.

Shortly after arriving at this realization, however, I suddenly felt a really cold feeling overshadow me, followed by an inexplicable emotion of desperately needing to return to this Lady. And most unexpectedly, I was then overwhelmed by an experience which led me to feel an intense love for Her, just as I was beginning to walk back to where this Lady was still standing. I honestly felt as though I really loved Her, even though I didn't know exactly who this mysterious Lady was at the time. But I knew one thing for sure and without a doubt - that I really needed to be in as close proximity to this Lady as physically possible.

And as soon as I had returned to my original spot behind the counter, this Lady most surprisingly turned to face me. She leaned over the counter and stared into my eyes, which caused me to feel slightly uncomfortable, but this uncomfortable feeling soon turned into a form of fear since She just stared into my eyes, intently for a while and consequently, I became afraid. But I was not afraid of this Lady per se but rather, as a result of the fact that it was as though She had the ability to look deep into my soul, and this frightened me somewhat. It was as though She could see straight through me.

And then I arrived at the realization that I was also afraid of the way in which She had looked at me, in my dream, and the expression that She wore on Her face at the time. This Lady's face was so close to mine, in fact, that all I could see were Her eyes and the top of Her cheeks. I noticed nothing else, and I could see nothing else. She continued to stare at me, always with the same expression on Her face.

I strongly felt as though she had something to tell me, but She refrained because either I wasn't ready to hear it, or I wouldn't be able to handle it.

This Lady remained silent throughout. However, I did notice that the expression on Her face was that of concern and unhappiness. And it was at this moment that I realized that Her eyes had suddenly become large and the wrinkles that I had previously seen on Her face, had completely disappeared. She was no longer old, but had become young.

Her eyes were the most beautiful shade of blue that I had ever seen before; they were so lovely that I find it difficult to express their beauty in words. And it was at this point in my dream that I suddenly came to the realization that this Lady, whom I had initially thought was a cute old Nun was, in fact, Our Lady, the Mother of God. She had finally revealed Herself to me and I knew, without a doubt, exactly who She was now.

Regrettably, all I had managed to say to Her at this point in my dream was that, "You are so beautiful!" And as soon as I had said these words to the Immaculate Virgin Mary, She suddenly turned to leave. Whilst She was only a short distance away, however, I watched Our Lady climb up a couple of invisible steps, and ascend into the sky before disappearing into real clouds. And I never saw Her in person again.

Walking over to the place where she had last stood before disappearing into the clouds, I fell to my knees, crying. Emotionally, I was most distraught and I remember saying to myself, "I didn't tell Her that I love Her."

And it was at this point in time that I suddenly awoke from my dream.

I was shocked when I realized that I was actually kneeling on my bed. Tears were streaming down my face, and I was trembling. My entire body was shaking, and I was absolutely terrified. I looked around my bedroom, and at the clock. It was 5 am in the morning. My husband was fast asleep since it was still dark outside, but I was so stricken with fear, panic and traumatism that I literally didn't know what to do next.

When I awoke from my dream, I knew, without a doubt, that the loud booming voice that I had heard coming from Heaven was, in fact, the voice of St Michael Archangel, the Prince and Leader of the Nine Choirs of Angels and of the Heavenly Hosts, who always announces the arrival of Our Lady.

My body just couldn't seem to stop shaking. In desperation, I woke up my husband and told him what had just happened to me, and all about my dream. I was still trembling uncontrollably the entire time that I was informing Sam about my dream, and I remember repeatedly asking my husband, "What am I going to do?" And I only managed to finally stop shaking after a considerable length of time had passed, and I was able to calm down somewhat.

At this stage, I failed to understand why this dream had occurred. I didn't know why Our Lady had chosen to appear to someone like me, a sinner and a lowly creature who was undoubtedly most unworthy of receiving a visit from the Immaculate Virgin Mary. I didn't know or understand how to interpret this dream. I simply failed to understand why the Mother of God had chosen to appear to me in the first place, and I was beside myself with grief, anxiety, alarm, dread, trepidation and dismay.

For months and years afterwards, I often thought about my dream. But what had always perturbed me the most was the way in which the Mother of God had stared directly, and most deeply, into my soul. I constantly felt as though there was something really important that the Queen of Heaven and of the Angels had wished to tell me, but for some reason, the Immaculate Virgin Mary had remained silent throughout my dream, and the purpose of Her visit had completely escaped me.

My name is Linda Virage, and I'd like to take this opportunity to tell you a story - a true story, a story about my life. They say that truth is stranger than fiction, and I never really understood this until I looked back at my own life and realized this idiom to be true.

This story is based on facts, and nothing but the truth. It's a personal story about great suffering, survival and personal triumph. It's the story of how I tenaciously overcame each and every one of the tremendous obstacles that were continuously and relentlessly being thrown in my path.

At this point, I would like to emphasize that all of the names in this book have been changed to protect the identities of the people being mentioned in this story.

And to give you a more detailed insight into my life from my childhood until adulthood, I shall start from the very beginning, my early childhood days.

I grew up in a relatively affluent middle-class neighbourhood with my parents and older sibling, Penelope. But I had no way of knowing, as a child, and no inkling at the time that I would be so blessed and privileged to be able to experience countless visions, religious dreams and spiritual experiences as a young adult and all the way through to middle age.

My parents emigrated from Europe to Australia in their mid-twenties. I was born and grew up in post-war Australia along with many other European immigrants. We were actually labelled as being 'Wogs' at the time because according to the 'Australians' whose parents were born in Australia, unlike mine, we were not true 'Aussies', and my sibling and I were teased at school, as a result. The other children perceived us to be different to them, and treated us accordingly.

When Penelope and I were young, our parents' English was very limited. Since they were of European descent, English was not my first language as a child. I did learn to speak English in kindergarten, however, and at school.

My earliest memories of being a student in kindergarten were the problems that I encountered whilst eating apples. My kindergarten teacher would prepare a fruit platter as a snack for all of the children in her class on a daily basis. But whenever I would eat a slice of apple, I would almost choke on the apple skin. For some unknown reason, I just couldn't seem to swallow apple skin properly without gagging first! So, my mother asked my kindergarten teacher if she could remove the apple skin before serving the apple pieces to me! How embarrassing is that!

And now, just to give you a bit of background information, I would like to firstly discuss my father and inform you of what he was actually like, not only as a person in general, but as a father figure too.

When my father was still a single man in his mid-twenties and in search of a wife and lifelong partner, he actually met my mother at a ball\dinner dance. They soon married, and started a tumultuous life together.

My mother's parents, who were both of European descent, had also emigrated from Europe to Australia in pursuit of a better life.

When Penelope and I were both young, our father was the most dominant person in our family.

He prided himself on his great muscular physique, particularly in relation to his muscly arms which he had naturally gained from working hard as a carpenter on the job. My father would occasionally encourage me, as a young child, to stand on his biceps to prove how strong he was to me! I was so impressed by the strength and size of the muscles on his arms, and I was in absolute awe of how strong my father really was at the time!

My father was extremely strict both as a father and as a parent in terms of our upbringing.

Although he was a harsh man in his younger days, I always knew that my father loved my sibling and I in his own way.

As mentioned earlier, he was a carpenter by trade and my father worked very hard on various building sites throughout his working life. He would leave for work early in the morning and return home early in the afternoon, exhausted and often quite grumpy from a hard day's work. My father expected dinner to be ready, and on the table, as soon as he arrived home and afterwards, my father would often go outside and engage himself in some gardening activities which was a form of relaxation for him, until the evening fell. He would then come inside, retire to the living room, sometimes falling asleep in his chair whilst engaging in a power nap, and watch some television before retiring early for the night, making sure that he was well-rested and ready for work the following day.

My father would always try to work six days a week because he loved earning the extra money that weekend work would bring. And although he earned a good wage, my father was very tight with his money, and it gave him great pleasure to watch his nest egg grow in the bank. He was obsessed with securing large sums of money in term deposits in an attempt to gain the most interest from his savings.

Since our father was so tight with his money, my sibling and I would often be scolded by our father if we were to accidentally leave the light on in our bedrooms due to the wastage of electricity involved, and the extra utility costs accumulated that he envisaged would occur as a result of our actions.

Penelope and I were never allowed to play with balls in the house, including really soft balls due to the supposed dints that the balls were making in the walls of the house and to the plaster, according to my father. Even as a child, I knew that using soft balls in the house could not possibly cause dints in the walls, and I could never understand my father's reasoning behind his logic!

My father was so strict as a parent that I will now give you an example to prove my point. My father was a very social man, and he would really enjoy a good chat with his friends. My father would often invite his friends over to our house and they would all gather around the kitchen table, in the adjacent room, and chew the fat together.

Meanwhile, Penelope and I were bored during these times so we would watch television together in the lounge room, either by ourselves or with the visitors' children if they happened to be around our age group, and had accompanied their parents in coming over to our house.

Our father would always make a point of rushing into the lounge room, peering at whatever program was currently being shown on television at the time, and he would ask us in a really stern voice as to what we were watching, and if it was appropriate viewing or not. He did not approve of us watching any programs on television that were deemed to contain adult themes, even as teenagers.

When Penelope and I were in our late teens and early twenties, our father always reinforced the importance of getting an education before finding a boyfriend. And he was never happy when my sibling and I went out with our friends for the evening.

It would be fair to say that my sibling and I led a rather sheltered life and that we had a very strict upbringing, as mentioned earlier. Although our father never displayed any physical violence towards us, Penelope and I were afraid of him nevertheless, particularly when he yelled at us.

Therefore, as both children and teenagers, my sibling and I never dared to rebel against him. We always felt compelled to comply with his wishes out of fear of suffering the consequences of our actions if we didn't comply.

My mother, on the other hand, was a photographer and often worked shift hours. She preferred to spend her own money on us rather than use my father's money to compensate for our needs, especially since my father gained little pleasure in spending his own money. He spent his hard-earned cash usually only on essentials like food, utilities, occasional holidays and educational expenses. However, my sibling and I both attended public schools for most of our schooling years. He was always afraid (more like terrified) of getting injured at work which would have the effect of terminating his ability to earn an income in which case our family would have to rely solely on his savings alone to cover all of our living expenses.

But I wasn't happy when my mother worked. I really missed her around the house. I often felt as though I didn't see her very much, and whenever I complained about not being able to spend enough time with her, my mother would continually respond to my pleas by citing the same thing, over and over again – she would reiterate how much she enjoyed working and loved earning the extra income for us.

My grandmother (our mother's mother) had been placed in charge of looking after my sibling and I whilst our mother worked. I loved my grandmother dearly, and I absolutely adored her. My grandmother would often walk me to school in the mornings and she would look after me in the evenings. In a way, she was like my second mother.

But the problem was that there was often much tension in the air when my grandmother spent time at our household, especially since my father and grandmother did not get along. In fact, they disliked each other immensely, and even to the point of loathing each other.

I think that my grandmother always believed that my father was unlike her own husband who was an extremely kind, compassionate and gentle soul before he had died from complications arising from a pig's valve heart transplant operation in his early sixties.

I don't really have very fond memories of my childhood. I was not an 'unhappy child', but I was a victim of my circumstances and of the environment in which I grew up in. It was just how my life was at the time, and I didn't really know any better. And this, in a sense, is where my story really begins.

# CHAPTER 1

I didn't really enjoy going to primary school very much, mainly because I was bullied on a regular basis. I was, what you would term, a 'goody-goody' at school, and I was the perfect target for school bullies. I don't know exactly what it was about me, in particular, but I seemed to be a bully magnet and I attracted bullies like bees to honey!

There are certain events that occurred during my schooling days which will be etched in my memory forever, but not in a good way. And even though these certain events took place more than forty years ago now, I strongly believe that I have still managed to retain these memories because they were so hurtful to me at the time. I must admit that it is rather difficult to forget experiences that hurt you more than words can express, but I will now spend some time in giving you a few examples of exactly what I mean.

During lunch time at school, one day, I was just standing on the asphalt basketball court, minding my own business, when suddenly, from across the other side of the court, I heard a boy shouting as loudly as he could, "Elephant!" Gazing in the direction of where I had last heard the voice coming from, I was shocked to see a boy that I knew, named Colin, staring directly at me.

I turned around to see if there was anyone else near me that he could have been talking to but there was nobody else in the vicinity of where I was standing, only me. I suddenly felt my cheeks turn red from embarrassment. Being called an 'elephant' was so incredibly humiliating and degrading.

Another child in this situation might have envisaged themselves being an elephant and charging towards Colin, like a bull, and tossing him into the air with their trunk, right out of the school grounds! But realistically, I found myself wishing that the Earth would swallow me up, and that I'd simply vanish into thin air.

Admittedly, I was rather overweight as a child. I had a bulging stomach which was quite noticeable and as a result, I suffered the consequences of carrying extra weight as a child at school. But I was always so hungry, and I simply loved food so very much! And it didn't help that my mother often made delicious desserts at home which were very high in calories, and I ate tons of meat and potatoes at dinner time! My father was a meat and potatoes man, and he wasn't keen on including too many vegetables in his diet!

In the end, however, I chose to ignore Colin's degrading remark, pretending that his most hurtful comment had not been specifically directed at me.

Unfortunately, Kerrie was another one of my 'bullies' whom I would now like to discuss in some detail. I was petrified of Kerrie, and I certainly had good reason to fear her! Kerrie was actually a pupil in my class at school, but she would often leave and go 'walk about' during class time without gaining permission from the classroom teacher first.

Kerrie was an extremely disruptive child, and didn't appear to be interested in learning anything at all at school.

One day, whilst I was busy focusing on completing my school work, totally oblivious to the usual classroom chatter of my classmates, I suddenly heard this almighty sound which gave me such a fright that I almost jumped out of my skin.

Looking up, I saw Kerrie in the corridor with blood oozing out of her hand. Bewildered, I just sat there in shock for a while, terrified. I soon realized that Kerrie had actually placed her fist through the top classroom window pane, and that she had punched the glass so hard that it had shattered into a number of pieces. I had no idea as to why Kerrie had done this, although I did assume that she must have had some quite severe anger management issues at the time!

And after the occurrence of this incident, I became even more afraid of Kerrie. And what made matters worse, was knowing that I was actually one of her bullying targets! I would always try to keep my distance from her, but I soon realized that this was not always a possibility.

After swallowing the last mouthful of my sandwich whilst finishing my lunch at my desk in the classroom, I stood up to leave but was shocked to see Kerrie just standing there, glaring at me. I immediately panicked, and felt my heart pounding in fright.

Frantically looking around the classroom and out into the corridor, I quickly scanned the area for a teacher or anyone else, for that matter. But I soon realized that there was no one in sight whom I could call upon for help. I stared at Kerrie in terror as she made her way towards me, edging closer and closer, like an animal preparing to attack its prey. I felt like I was a fly caught in a spider web with no way of being able to escape from my predicament.

And it was then that Kerrie kicked me, as hard as she possibly could, in the knee. Too afraid to retaliate, I managed to escape from the classroom, much to my relief, and out into the safety of the playground where there were actual teachers around who were on duty at the time.

I am thinking that the term 'helicopter mum' was created in honour of my mother! Eating my lunch in the classroom at school was a task that I dreaded and feared on a daily basis! My mother usually packed me a sandwich filled with salami and green capsicum for lunch which was most unfortunate for me, since the filling would emit a really strong smell that would quickly disperse around the classroom and attract unwanted attention on my part, from the other children. Often, I was teased as a result of the odour of my sandwiches. And to the others in my class, the stench was pungent!

Eating food at school that was brought from home was anything but a pleasurable experience, and always caused me to feel most uncomfortable and awkward. I really didn't want to be 'different' to the other children at my school, and I certainly never wished to 'stand out from the crowd'. All I ever really wanted so desperately was to fit in with the other children, but my mother's actions prevented me from being able to do so.

I would even resort to begging my mother not to give me such 'smelly' lunches, and ask her if she could pack me cheese and vegemite sandwiches as an alternative, which is what many of the other children brought to school for lunch. But my mother reiterated that she simply could not give me sandwiches of this nature because she would feel too sorry for me to have to eat such bland sandwiches for lunch, as I had suggested, and she always absolutely insisted that I bring gourmet sandwiches to school instead! As a result, she continued to give me salami and capsicum or bacon and capsicum sandwiches for lunch and of course, the bullying continued on a regular basis and only escalated to a more intense level.

It's important to note here, however, that children who bring gourmet lunches to school in today's society are the envy of every child! School life was extremely different when I was a child to that of society today.

I would now like to discuss another stark example of how my mother's actions contributed to my being bullied at school. And during these times, I would simply be playing with my friends at lunchtime when suddenly, my mother would appear in the playground holding a change of clothes, as a consequence of the weather either becoming colder or warmer during the day whilst I was at school, and I often wondered how she could embarrass me like this! The problem was that if a change in temperature occurred and the weather suddenly become cooler, for instance, she would bring me some warmer clothes to change into so that I wouldn't be cold playing outside at school during lunchtime. To be perfectly honest, I would much rather have received frostbite in the playground than be teased by the other children for suddenly appearing in the classroom after lunchtime to be wearing a completely different set of clothes to what I was wearing when I had initially arrived at school, as if by magic!

Furthermore, on another occasion, this time during recess, however, whilst I was playing nicely with a small group of friends, I looked up into the distance, by chance, and saw my mother marching into the schoolgrounds, like a soldier on a mission, holding her trusty broom under her arm, as she headed towards me. I couldn't help but to cringe at the sight of her intrusion, and my friends just stared at me in disbelief. How could I possibly explain this to them since there were no words to justify my mother's actions? Dumbfounded, I felt more embarrassed, during these times, than I can ever possibly hope to express in words.

But my mother always had a rationale for her most unusual behaviour, and it didn't matter how much I pleaded with her to at least try to behave more like the other parents at school, she simply ignored my pleas and continued to embarrass me at school on a regular basis.

Penelope was terrified of spiders, as was I (and I still am, for that matter!) and on the rare occasion when there were Daddy-long-legs spiders hiding in the girls' toilets, my sibling would inform my mother immediately after school that day that she was too afraid to go to the toilet due to the unwelcome inhabitants.

And so, the following day, my mother would get rid of all of the spiders in the girls' toilets with her broom, so that we could enter the girls' toilets again, without fear!

A most unusual bullying incident happened during my lunchtime break at school, one afternoon, which still baffles me even to this day, as to why it actually occurred in the first place. But in this instance, my mother was not to blame, nor did I ever do anything wrong, for that matter. I was never actually mean to anyone in order to be able to justify the actions of the bullies who targeted me, since it was just not in my nature to bully others or even to say one unkind word to anyone.

I was sitting on top of some monkey bars in the school playground, minding my own business, when I suddenly noticed a group of secondary school girls walking across the oval and heading my way. The group of girls came right up to me and one of them, most unexpectedly, pushed me off the top of the monkey bars and I fell to the ground, landing on the hard concrete surface below. I began to cry. Baffled, I immediately went to report this incident to the school principal. Apparently, the secondary school girl who had pushed me off the play equipment had a younger sister named Jane who attended my school. But what made this situation so perplexing to me was that Jane was actually one of my close friends whom I had always treated with kindness. I just wasn't capable of bullying anyone ever.

However, one of the girls in my small circle of friends, named Margaret, had actually teased Jane earlier and I have no idea as to why Jane's older sister had bullied me over this incident when I had done absolutely nothing wrong. I was not the culprit here, but only an innocent victim under the circumstances.

Anyway, moving on to my teenage years, my secondary school experiences were not much better than my primary ones. Again, I was bullied but, this time, I was mainly bullied by the same group of girls who belonged to the 'in-crowd'. At both recess and lunch time, they would often gather together in the girls' toilets and smoke cigarettes. I was always afraid to enter these toilets in case I found them in there smoking and if I happened to see them, I would immediately back track and leave, even if I was absolutely busting to go to the toilet and I would try again later, hoping that they had left so that I could relieve myself in peace!

During my home economics class at school, whilst I was busy cleaning up, this same group of girls would bully me. They had essentially chosen to target me for their bulling behaviour, and would pour some dishwashing detergent into my cooking, giggling simultaneously in doing so. Unfortunately, this particular group of girls made a habit of doing this to me on a regular basis and to this day, I actually don't know if they knew that I was aware of their actions but nevertheless, their bullying behaviour had the effect of upsetting me beyond words. And when I took my cooking home afterwards, my mother would always want to try the food that I had made at school because it looked and smelled so delicious. So, I was continually compelled to dissuade her from eating the food that I had made and was forced to tell her the truth, as a result.

It was during times like these that I became extremely distressed about being the constant target of their pranks and bullying practices. Personally, it made me feel so awful that my mother couldn't try my cooking. But I was simply too afraid to tell the home economics teacher the truth about this group of girls in case they bullied me to an even greater extent for telling the teacher on them.

Furthermore, I was also bullied during my PE classes which I absolutely dreaded and loathed since the teacher would often choose two Captains for sporting activities and the most popular children in my class were always chosen to be Captains.

I was never given the same opportunities as they were given, simply due to the fact that I was not popular at school. I was a painfully shy student who was already beginning to lack in self-confidence and self-esteem due to the relentless bullying and personal attacks that were continually being directed at me.

In relation to those students who were chosen to be sports Captains, however, they were instructed, by the teacher, to stand at the front of the class and call out the names of their team members.

But what made matters even worse was that I would never hear my name being called, not even once, by either of the two Captains. I was always the last student in the class to be left standing all by myself. And during these moments, I would feel so alone, embarrassed, uncomfortable and uneasy, since no one wanted me to join their team.

But despite being bullied at school, I didn't allow these negative experiences to deter me from enjoying my secondary schooling years since I really loved acquiring knowledge and learning new things. And the bullying only encouraged me to work even harder at school, causing me to push myself to the maximum so as to excel at as many subjects as I possibly could under the circumstances.

Although my confidence and self-esteem were dwindling as a result of the relentless bullying attacks and I often berated myself for being such a shy and quiet individual (for I had always wished, deep down, that I was a confident and popular student at school), I prided myself instead, on achieving the highest grades possible that I knew I was capable of attaining, as compensation for the negative personality traits that I perceived myself to possess.

But one thing was clear to me from a very young age - I really didn't like myself at all. I thought that I was unattractive, and I would always focus on the negative aspects of my personality and physical appearance as opposed to the positive. And looking back, I find it quite sad that this is how I actually perceived myself as a teenager, and that I carried this view of myself all the way through to adulthood and for more than half of my life.

# CHAPTER 2

You may be thinking that my childhood sounds like it was rather depressing and quite miserable. Yet, I rarely became depressed. I was still a rather happy child whilst growing up, and I would just carry on with my life and go with the flow whereas Penelope was the exact opposite of me.

I didn't really have any high expectations as a child which also seemed to have the effect of lessening the chance of my experiencing disappointments in life.

On weekends, my mother would often drop Penelope and I at our cousins' house. My auntie (my mother's sister) had three sons – the eldest, Brendon, was only one year older than Penelope. The middle child, Thomas, was my age, and the youngest, Troy, was considerably younger than me.

I never felt at ease whilst visiting my auntie's house. She was a very cold woman, and the total opposite in nature to that of my mother. I often wondered how they could be sisters. She would talk to Penelope and I in a most unfriendly and rather icy tone, and I always felt as though she didn't like us. My uncle treated us in much the same way.

Thomas never wanted anything to do with me. I always felt that he was ashamed to be seen with me, and he never made an effort to play with or even talk to me, for that matter. So, I always had to tag along with Brendon and Penelope, and hang out with them because Thomas had rejected me from very early on. I failed to understand why he never wanted to have anything to do with me but in the past, I had always suspected that it was because I was a 'goody-goody'; he smoked cigarettes from an early age, and was the total opposite in nature to me. I have never even tried a cigarette in my entire life nor any other form of drugs, for that matter.

Whenever my entire family were invited to my auntie's house for dinner, although she was a really good cook, we were always afraid to eat our fill because, in my view, my auntie was very stingy with food! If she was serving us potatoes, for instance, she would go so far as to ask each one of us, in turn, what size potato we would like to eat– small or large! But when my parents invited my auntie, uncle and cousins over for dinner, the opposite scenario was true!

My uncle would sit down at our dinner table, loosen his belt and inform us that he had not eaten anything all day long so that he could tuck into the feast that my parents had prepared for them!

My auntie and uncle did not really like my father. They tolerated him, but I was always under the impression that they thought that he was beneath them because he was a carpenter and my uncle worked for a most prestigious university, even though he wasn't a lecturer nor did he hold a high-ranking position there.

Every morning, my uncle ate breakfast like a king which his wife neatly prepared and laid out for him. His breakfast strongly resembled the type of breakfast that would be served to guests staying in a 5-star hotel! In general, his behaviour was in accordance with someone who is a really important person in life and in my opinion, my uncle could be categorized as being a swank.

I will never forget the time that my father, Penelope and I went away on vacation with my auntie, uncle and cousins to a beautiful seaside location. My grandmother also accompanied us on the holiday to help look after my sibling and I since my mother had to work and was unable to join us.

However, my poor grandmother became extremely upset when, whilst sightseeing as a group, my uncle proceeded to buy ice-creams for all of his children including himself, but failed to ask my grandmother, as well as my sibling and I, if we would like an ice-cream too.

My grandmother told me afterwards how upset she was that my uncle had not even considered asking us if we had wanted an ice-cream. I had always believed that it was the principle of the matter that was of crucial importance to my grandmother, and that this was the reasoning behind why she had become so upset in the first place.

One morning, whilst still away on vacation, my cousins excitedly ran up to my sibling and I and told us that their father had hired a boat by the river, and that they would soon be going on a boat ride. Our uncle had not invited Penelope and I to join them, nor was my grandmother invited, for that matter. I distinctly remember being extremely upset that we could not go with them to enjoy a river boat cruise with my cousins.

I don't really have very fond memories of the times that I spent away on vacation with my family growing up.

Furthermore, I never really felt as though I grew up in an environment surrounded by loving family members and relatives. And although my father would often tell me that he loved me, and I really believe that he did love me in his own special way, he used to fondly call me by a nickname which I really didn't like at the time and this word, when translated into English, meant 'cannon'. He basically addressed me by this nickname because he said that I was 'solid like a cannon' since I was actually quite overweight as a child, as mentioned earlier in this book.

But I failed to consider this to be a very flattering nickname and, in my view, it was quite derogatory and insulting to be constantly called by this nickname whilst growing up. My father would also make jokes about how much food I could eat at dinner time.

Although he did actually have a sense of humour, the problem was that my father's jokes were usually directed at the expense of others rather than at himself, and so his personal jokes were quite insulting and hurtful in the presence of others.

Thinking back, it's really no wonder that I began to develop an inferiority complex at a very young age which continued on throughout adulthood.

I would like to change the focus now and discuss the relationship that existed between my sibling and I as children growing up together.

As a child, I was always very playful, and I had a really vivid imagination which I now attribute to being a gift from God that He bestowed upon me. Although I had an older sibling, I often played by myself, however – I would either play with my dolls, engage in completing puzzles, word searches, or even do some colouring in. I would often play with my neighbours' children, ride my bike outside or play with my pets.

Time and time again, I would ask Penelope to play board games with me, but she would usually decline my repeated invitations. Her response would nearly always be the same, however, and she would say things like, "You know I don't like playing games," each and every time I pleaded with her to play with me.

It's hard to believe but my sibling would actually sit and watch me play by myself, rather than join me. I don't think that she really knew how to play imaginative games. Penelope was so very different in personality and in nature to me.

Penelope would always take school and her education most seriously, even whilst she was a student in primary school!

My sibling fretted about her marks and academic performance from a very young age and she would, more often than not, rather complete her homework than engage in free play as a child.

I have always really loved animals, and felt the need to own some pets. They were my constant and loyal companions, and always showed me love and loyalty in return for mine.

I found it most unusual behaviour, on her part, that although Penelope seemed to really like our pets, she rarely had any involvement with them at all; she seemed to prefer to watch me playing with our animals instead.

But my grandmother was my only true best friend. I have extremely fond memories of her looking after me whilst my mother worked. I really loved my grandmother; she was so wonderful to me, and was continually so supportive and encouraging of me. I was extremely close to my grandmother, and I always really respected her opinion. She often made the time to play board games with me like 'Snakes and Ladders', when no one else would. Strangely enough, I always managed to somehow win the game!

Often, our grandmother would spend her own hard-earned money on buying Penelope and I the most beautiful toys and gifts. She was so generous with money, and was always extremely loving with my sibling and I.

I truly believed that I had the best grandmother in the world, and I appreciated her more than words can ever hope to express.

She also taught me how to make delicious cakes and desserts, and I became really good at kneading dough and making pastries, as a result of her wonderful guidance and instruction.

My grandmother would give me advice on so many different matters, and I was always in awe of her common sense and wisdom. In my view, she was like a wise old owl who possessed a wealth of knowledge and information about so many different and vast topics. I really enjoyed her company and listening to the interesting stories about her life as a child growing up in a communist country, and in relation to her husband who sadly died before I was born, at a time when my grandmother was only aged in her fifties.

Together, my grandmother and I made a great team, both in cooking and when playing board games. I truly feel so blessed to have had such a wonderful grandmother who loved me most sincerely and unconditionally until the day she passed away, only one month short of reaching her Ninetieth Birthday.

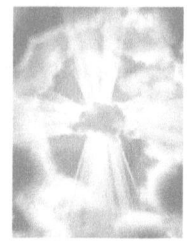

# CHAPTER 3

Both of my parents were Roman Catholics, and we would often go to Church on Sundays as a family. I never complained about going to Church, and it just became a significant part of our family routine.

My mother and grandmother were both very religious, as was I. It was quite natural for me to ask God for His help if I really needed or wanted something, and to give thanks afterwards when my prayers were answered. Praying and talking to God was always second nature to me.

If I was ever in trouble or needed some assistance in life, I would never hesitate to ask God for His help. After all, I have always believed that God can do anything, and that nothing is impossible through God.

But what I have come to realize is that a belief in God is not really enough on its own but rather, it's a combination of believing that nothing is impossible through God together with possessing a belief in God's existence which is of the utmost importance here in order for miracles to be able to occur in our everyday lives. And if we possess even a small amount of faith, the size of a mustard seed, in fact, then we shall be able to move mountains that have suddenly appeared in our path as a result of our faith and belief in God.

Although I have been religious for almost all of my life, my earliest recollection of first becoming spiritual was at the age of about six years.

Ever since I can remember, next to the bed in my bedroom on the wall, on my right-hand side, hung the most beautiful and extremely large painting (which now hangs in the loungeroom of my house for my entire family to enjoy and be able to view on a daily basis) of a Guardian Angel, who is standing behind two children, as their Protector. The young boy and girl are about to retrieve a ball which is caught in a tree branch which hangs delicately over of the edge of the bank of a winding stream which meanders through smooth rocks. The Guardian Angel, who has magnificently large white feathery wings, has both arms outstretched in front of them, and is standing behind the two children, getting ready to lay one hand directly over the head of each child in order to protect them from falling into the stream upon retrieval of the ball.

I distinctly remember gazing upon this beautiful painting as a child, and absolutely loving this picture, especially the idea of having a Guardian Angel who protects us from harm and always has our safety and well-being at heart.

I also have very sad but fond memories simultaneously of playing by myself on the floor, next to the bed, in my extremely small bedroom. I often played with my tea set and Barbie doll who was dressed like a ballerina and whom I had named Cindy. I would often pretend that my Barbie doll was an Angel and using my hands to fly her through the air, I would ask Cindy if she would come and fly with me and we would soar to different locations together, in my imagination.

It's interesting to note here, at this point in time, that I had actually believed in the presence of Angels from an extremely young age.

At the age of fifteen, I remember studying diligently for my first mathematics exam at secondary school. I was in Year 10 at the time, and maths was definitely not my forte. I was much better at English and the languages, and I was most concerned about the possibility of failing this exam at the time.

As a most conscientious academic student, I was extremely studious and always tried my utmost to perform as well as I possibly could in tests, exams and school work in general. I never really considered myself to be an ace at problem solving, although I wasn't keen on giving up when struggling to work out the solution to a particular problem, however.

Writing was my forte and I always loved English the most as a subject at school including writing narratives as well as essays in any genre, for that matter.

I was fortunate enough to be able to have my own study room at home and just above the doorway, on the wall, was a wooden cross of Jesus Christ. I remember staring at this Cross often, and praying to Jesus to help me to do well in my upcoming mathematics exam.

On the day of the exam, I felt rather nervous but once I began working on the exam paper, I must admit that I was quite surprised at how easy I was actually finding it. And no one was more shocked than I was when my teacher announced in front of the entire class that I had achieved the second highest ranking in the mathematics exam in the Year 10 cohort! This was so unlike me, especially for maths, and I immediately knew that Jesus had assisted me with my exam that day, and that He had answered my prayers.

This significant event in my teenage years ignited a spark in my soul, enhancing my spiritual journey. And over the coming years, my supernatural and general life experiences both strengthened and solidified my faith overall, as well as my strong belief in God which was re-established over and over again, each and every time my prayers were answered during my lifetime.

Three weeks before my final Year 12 exams, I suddenly contracted strep throat and became quite ill, as a result. I remember having severe muscle aches and pains, feeling exhausted and struggling to study for my exams efficiently.

My GP (General Practitioner) gave me a course of extremely strong antibiotics to take before recovering from my illness.

Nevertheless, I was most grateful to God when I passed my Year 12 exams in all subjects, despite the challenges that I faced during my illness.

At the completion of Year 12 and my HSC (Higher School Certificate), I enrolled in a business course but discontinued my studies shortly after commencement as soon as I realized that studying business subjects in general was just not my forte.

After having undertaken a week of work experience at a primary school, this effectively ignited in me a strong desire to become a teacher and so, I applied to get into a number of primary teaching courses in my home town for the following year, as a result.

I genuinely enjoyed the company of younger children, and I had such a great rapport with children of primary school age. I simply loved listening to their stories in passing conversation, as well as learning about their many different life experiences. Young children are so innocent, honest and impressionable.

I was simply ecstatic at being accepted into a Bachelor of Education (Primary) course at a local university. And as soon as I had begun my primary teaching training, I immediately knew that I had made the right career choice.

In my first year, I received a two-year HECS (Higher Education Contribution Scheme) scholarship without having even applied for one due to the fact that I was excelling in my course. Being awarded this scholarship basically meant that I was exempt from paying university fees for the first two years of my course.

But once I had completed my course, I had the arduous task of looking for employment which I found most difficult because at the time, there was an oversupply of primary school teachers since they had recently been recruited from oversees to teach in Australia. And although I had excelled in my course, I was not prepared to teach in the country where there were more employment opportunities available.

I had always resided amidst an urban population for all of my life, and I possessed a real phobia of snakes and spiders. Therefore, I was consistently more at ease walking on suburban footpaths than in bushland. I reasoned that at least whilst on a paved surface, I could always notice a creepy crawly that was making its way towards me, or if I was about to step on a snake!

So eventually, I gave up on finding employment as a teacher, and I found a part-time job at a women's hospital in the Public Relations

Department. I was assigned my own office and although it was only tiny, I still really loved my office as well as my new job. Basically, I was hired to help raise money to re-equip the hospital's Special Care Nursery and although I was only paid a part-time salary, I worked full-time hours. I really enjoyed my job, and even the other employees thought that I was paid as a full-time employee. But I was just so happy to actually be employed in the work force rather than be an unemployed teacher, and I really did enjoy being busy at work. It gave me real purpose in life at the time.

As I became older, I started to become more and more anxious about the prospect of being unable to find a husband and lifelong partner. I was never really ambitious, and my great ambition in life, at the time, was to get married and have as many children as possible. And so, as soon as I began to realize that my dream in life may never be realized, I started to panic and became extremely unhappy, as a result.

However, as time passed, I wondered how I would ever be able to find a suitable partner in life. I had already met quite a few different 'potential candidates', but I could never envisage myself long-term with any of them, let alone as a life partner.

So, I began praying to God to help me find a suitable husband. I prayed for Him to find me, first and foremost, a religious man, which was at the top of my list, a Roman Catholic like myself, a good and kind man, and an Italian looking man, since I was most attracted to men who have dark coloured hair which was in contrast to mine.

And I waited and waited for my prayers to be answered but slowly,

I began to wonder if my petitions to God would ever be granted and if my dream would come true at some time in the future.

# CHAPTER 4

I was rather close to my mother, in particular, both as a teenager and adult, much closer to her than I ever was to my father anyway. I would never actually feel comfortable just sitting down and having a chat with my father since I was unable to talk with him in the same way that I could with my mother.

I also loved my mother dearly, and I always wished to spend as much time with her as possible, since we were quite similar in nature. My mother was also very religious, as was her mother, as mentioned earlier in this book.

One afternoon, as an adult in my twenties, whilst I was just relaxing in a chair and sitting at the dining room table, chatting with my mother just as we had done on a number of occasions before, we suddenly heard the front door swing open, on its own accord. Puzzled, I quickly headed towards the front door to close it again but, strangely enough, I felt no breeze coming through the open door, and it was definitely not a windy day. The trees outside did not appear to be moving at all. But what was most surprising to me was that our front door had two locks attached, one of them being a deadlock and so I could not imagine how our front door could have opened on its own without any form of human intervention. Although my mother and I were both very surprised at this strange occurrence, I soon dismissed this incident and after closing the front door most securely, I headed back to the kitchen to resume chatting with my mother.

After a short while had passed, however, my mother and I were both absolutely astonished when exactly the same thing happened again in succession. The front door suddenly swung open by itself but this time, I knew that I had previously definitely closed the front door very securely myself.

My mother and I looked upon this occurrence, as well as the previous door opening incident, as a supernatural sign which could be interpreted as doors opening in my life in the near future.

However, these two supernatural signs were closely followed by a third supernatural event, on the same day, whereby the radio suddenly turned on by itself and began blaring in the presence of my mother and I. We both got such a fright at the time since neither of us expected this to occur, nor were we standing near the radio at the time, and neither of us had actually turned on the radio either, for that matter. We just stared at each other in amazement, and I wondered whether this was a sign from God that an announcement would soon be made in my life.

And these three supernatural events occurred at a time in which I was most unhappy being single in life; I was praying constantly to God for His assistance, and I really hoped that something good was going to happen in my life in the near future which would bring me great happiness and joy. And I was right.

It's an interesting fact that many of my supernatural experiences actually occurred in the presence of my mother who has also been a most religious person for her entire life. Recently, my mother informed me of a story regarding a time when she was aged only about four years, whilst living in Europe with her parents during World War 2. After suddenly hearing the sirens blaring to alert people in their village that air strikes were about to hit their town, my mother's family all quickly huddled together in the underground bunker that her father had built for their safety and refuge from the bombings. My mother distinctly remembers saying to her parents and younger sister at the time, whilst in the midst of air strikes, "Don't worry, Hail Mary will save us." And my mother was right.

I was absolutely astounded when my mother recited this story to me. I was amazed that a mere four-year-old child could display such deep faith in Our Lady and was already aware that the Immaculate Virgin Mary was capable of saving my mother and her family in this most terrifying and dire situation.

My mother also told me an interesting story about my grandmother (my mother's mother) which I was most surprised to hear. Whilst still living in Europe, my grandmother had met a man who was eight years her senior and after she had fallen in love with him, she prayed to Saint Therese of Lisieux, 'The Little Flower' (who was her favourite Saint) for her help and intercession so that my grandmother could marry the man of her dreams. My mother then proceeded to tell me that Saint Therese actually appeared to my grandmother in a dream on one occasion and after her dream, my grandmother knew that she would marry my grandfather and that's exactly what she did! I really wish that I had known this fact earlier, however, as I would have questioned my grandmother about her dream in detail but unfortunately, I have lost this opportunity since my grandmother passed away over seventeen years ago now.

Whilst my sibling was completing her university exam for a post-graduate course that she was undertaking at the time, another unusual supernatural experience occurred, outside the university gates, whilst my mother and I were merely waiting for Penelope to complete her exam paper. Penelope was due to finish soon, and we were both praying that Penelope would do well and be able to pass this most important exam.

Suddenly, my mother and I gazed up into the vast blue sky, and we were both astonished to see a cloud which was shaped like an Angel. And what made this occurrence even more amazing was that there were no other clouds in the sky that could be seen at the time. I immediately knew that the sight of this Angel-shaped cloud meant that Penelope would pass her exam, and I was right. My sibling went on to achieve multiple degrees including her PhD, until finally reaching the pinnacle of her career in becoming an Associate Professor.

The spiritual experiences that have taken place in my life, although vast and many, were all quite different in nature, and always occurred intermittently and most unexpectedly.

For example, whilst working at the women's hospital, my department had organized a fundraising event, a hospital fete, which took place in the hospital car park, and all proceeds went towards purchasing new equipment for the Special Care Nursery. The Fundraising Department was represented at a special stall at the Fete, and I was positioned at a table near a large whiteboard which had brochures pinned to it informing the public about the Special Care Nursery at the hospital. I remember it being a particularly windy day and all of a sudden, without warning, a huge gust of wind blew the whiteboard into the back of my head at high force. It was actually the metal corner of the whiteboard that hit my head really hard and I just sat there for a while, stunned at the sequence of events that had just occurred. My manager, who had witnessed the entire incident, sent me home immediately. On the way home, however, I visited my doctor who carefully examined my head but failed to see any scratches or marks on my scalp, not even one.

So, after returning home, I lay down on the couch to rest for a while. But what I failed to mention earlier though was that my mother had also attended the Hospital Fete whilst I was working, since she loved to browse at knick-knacks at fetes and markets, in particular, and it was one of her favourite pastimes, in fact. But unbeknown to me at the time, my mother had found and bought, at one of the stalls, two religious pictures – one was a picture of Jesus, and the other was a picture of the Sacred Heart of Jesus and Our Lady. They were both really beautiful pictures, and I just stared at them whilst resting on the couch.

And suddenly, to my utter dismay, I received a really warm feeling whereby I felt so much happiness and joy at the time, but I had absolutely no idea as to why I was feeling this way. And this immensely warm and happy feeling lasted for quite some time. Consequently, I firmly believe that both Jesus and Our Lady had protected me from becoming hurt during my accident at work, since I was totally fine and suffered no injuries or trauma, as a result.

One cold afternoon, on a wet and dreary day, my mother and I decided to go for a walk around the block together. It was drizzling lightly, but I really felt the need to stretch my legs a little. And grabbing an umbrella each, we braved the weather and ventured outside to get some exercise. We had just reached the end of our street when something shiny in the gutter caught my eye. Taking a closer look, I realized that it was a silver Cross of Jesus but I continued to walk past, without stopping, due to the rain and bad weather.

But I had only walked past the Crucifix of Jesus, a few steps, when I suddenly stopped and thought to myself, "I can't just leave Jesus lying there in the gutter like this in the muddy water. He doesn't deserve this." And so, I quickly backtracked, and picked up the Cross of Jesus. I held it in my hand and squeezed it tightly so as not to drop the Cross.

I soon realized that it was a Cross that had obviously broken off somebody's Rosary, and there were only a few pale pink beads still attached to the broken Rosary chain.

When we arrived home, I washed the Cross of Jesus and really treasured it. This Crucifix was of most special significance to me because I had found it myself rather than having bought it at a shop. I loved it dearly and to this day, I still find this Cross of Jesus most precious and invaluable to me.

But I gave this most beautiful Cross of Jesus, that I truly treasured more than words can ever hope to express, away and to this day, I will miss being in possession of this most beautiful and priceless Crucifix of Jesus for the rest of my life.

# CHAPTER 5

My sibling used to travel to conferences overseas at least twice yearly. I was always concerned about her own personal safety during these times and so, I gave her the Crucifix that I had found in the gutter so that Jesus would always protect her during her travels. She loved the Cross, and always carried it with her in her handbag whenever she travelled.

But as soon as she had stopped travelling, I hinted that I really loved the Cross, she no longer needed its protection for travelling purposes, and that I would be most grateful if she could return the Crucifix to me since I was its rightful owner. Unexpectedly, however, my sibling seemed most reluctant to give it back, implying that she really loved the Cross. In the end though, Penelope did say that she would return it to me, if I really wanted the Cross back. But then, a feeling of guilt suddenly overshadowed me once she had admitted how much she actually loved the Cross, and I allowed her to keep it.

I was, by now, in my late twenties and still, there was no husband in sight. And what made matters worse was that I didn't even have a boyfriend, as yet, for that matter. I continued to work at the women's hospital, and to pray to God to find me a suitable husband. I had never expected to be still single at this age, and I began to wonder if I would ever get married and have children. I was running out of time, and I secretly began to panic again.

But God did answer my prayers, just as He always had in the past. And what was most remarkable and absolutely amazing to me, when I met the man of my dreams, was that he was exactly the type of man that I was looking for – he possessed the exact qualities that I had asked God to find for me – he was very religious, a Roman Catholic, of Italian descent, he had a great sense of humour and was an incredibly kind and good-natured man. His name was Sam, and he was introduced to me by a mutual acquaintance.

The first time that I actually set eyes upon him, I knew that this man definitely had the enormous potential to become my husband or at least my boyfriend. I had never met anyone quite like him before. We chatted and chatted during our first meeting, and I felt more comfortable talking to him than to any other man that I had previously met in the past. I wasn't shy around Sam; I wasn't afraid to talk to him, and I felt most comfortable in his presence really early on. Sam didn't feel like he was a total stranger to me, even though this is exactly what he was at the time.

Sam had twin sisters as well as a brother, and he spoke most fondly of his family which really impressed me. He was obviously very intelligent, and miraculously ticked all of the boxes for me.

So, we started dating, and saw each other at least once a week, at the very beginning of our relationship anyway. Sam treated me like a real princess, and I loved every minute of it! He was such a gentleman at all times. Sam even insisted on paying for everything when we went out on a date, and he bought me the most beautiful gifts which I really treasured.

For my 30th Birthday, Sam took me out on a date to see a musical and afterwards, we had dinner at a lovely restaurant. He also bought me the most beautiful long-stemmed red roses as a gift, in addition to a magnificent diamond necklace.

Sam was so romantic, as was I. He was generous, affectionate, compassionate and he had such a wonderful sense of humour, as mentioned earlier. Sam was really fun to be around. In my view, he was perfect in every way. I really enjoyed his company, and I just loved being around him continually.

My parents had met Sam a number of times already, and they both really liked him. I had also met Sam's parents, siblings, nephews and nieces. They had all made me feel so very welcome. His family were warm and friendly, and I liked them all very much. They seemed to be a really close family, as was mine.

After Sam and I had been going out together for a period of six months, he took me out on a date to a most beautiful park. We walked around the gardens holding hands, simply enjoying each other's company, and the warmth of the sun. The birds were chirping in the trees, and we stopped to rest at a most serene location in the park where there were a number of ducks swimming and paddling around in the pond. Sam had taken me to a most romantic setting and suddenly, my heart pounded with excitement as Sam bent down on one knee, and proposed to me. I was filled with joy, and I immediately replied, "YES!" without any form of hesitation whatsoever. Sam was so romantic! He was my soulmate, and I felt so blessed that God had brought him into my life. And now we were engaged to be married! In my heart, I knew that Sam and I were meant to be together, and that there was no other man on this entire earth who was more perfect for me, and who could make me happier, than Sam.

We planned our wedding day for the end of June; our wedding would take place in only four months' time. It would be winter then, but we didn't care as we were so keen to get married that we just couldn't wait any longer.

And it was whilst we were planning our wedding day that an enormous dilemma occurred in my life, and I made a decision which I came to regret later, and for which I blamed my father directly for many years to come. He somehow managed to ruin my life and my happiness at a time when I never thought that he ever would.

And this dilemma actually occurred after I had informed my father that Sam and I were engaged. My father seemed happy enough at hearing the news but then, he dropped a bombshell on me which I really didn't expect at the time.

My husband-to-be, before I had met him, had worked really hard in the IT industry. And with the money that he had earned from working over-time, he had decided to plan for the future by investing in properties.

My father, on the other hand, deposited large sums of money that he had earned into term deposits in the bank, rather than investing his money in buying real estate. Admittedly, Sam had accumulated a large mortgage as a result of buying investment properties, but he was receiving rental income to help offset his mortgage.

I was really proud of Sam for owning some investment properties and as a result, I felt the need to inform my father about his achievements. But regrettably, what I had failed to realize at the time was that in doing so, I had just made one of the biggest mistakes of my life for which I would berate myself afterwards for a number of years to come.

My father immediately went into a rage, and started yelling at me. He was terrified of the debt that Sam had already accumulated from his investment properties. In his view, we would never be able to repay this large debt back to the bank. So, in his rage, my father made a threat to me which I took most seriously at the time. He threatened that if Sam did not sell all of his properties immediately, then my father would not attend our wedding. I really wanted my father to be present at our wedding and so reluctantly, I asked Sam to sell all of his investment properties, which he actually did, just for me.

Most unfortunately, for Sam and I, the housing market was at its lowest point in decades at the time which is why Sam ended up making a loss at the auctions for the sale of his investment properties.

Sadly, however, within only a couple of years, the housing market recovered and selling the properties during that time would have resulted in us making a significant profit instead of a loss.

By selling his properties at a loss, as a result of my father's influence, Sam proved just how much he really loved me, without a doubt, at the time. But I will always wish that I had never told my father about Sam's investment properties in the first place, and that I had ignored my father's threat to not attend our wedding.

And even to this day, I truly regret having asked Sam to sell his properties before we got married because later in life, after we had built a new house together, there were times when we experienced real financial difficulties – times when we had failed to have enough income to pay our monthly mortgage repayments to the bank which could easily have resulted in us having to sell our house. But somehow, with God's help, we had always managed to retain our property, and not have to place it for sale on the market.

# CHAPTER 6

Looking back, I don't really understand why my father panicked at the time. We could have always sold one of Sam's properties if we found ourselves in real financial difficulties later on. Why sell the investment properties when we were not in any real financial trouble yet? And this was Sam's argument, as was mine. My father's logic didn't make any sense to either of us at all, and it was a huge contributing factor in ruining not only my life, but my entire family's life as well, forever.

And for years afterwards, although I still loved him, I think that deep down, I harboured some form of resentment towards my father for demanding that Sam sell his investment properties before we were married. At this point in time, I wish so much, even to this day, that I had enabled my father to carry out his threat of being absent from our wedding, and that we had retained Sam's investment properties instead.

And we have still never recovered financially from selling my husband's investment properties at a loss, so many years ago. If I had not asked Sam to sell all of his properties at the time, we would definitely not be in this position today, and this is something that I have to live with for the rest of my life, and somehow come to terms with.

But now, I would like to turn my attention back to our wedding preparations. It was only three weeks before my wedding day, and I was still working at the women's hospital. I had made the enormous mistake of getting my make-up done at a local shopping centre consecutively three times in total, before my actual wedding day, in an attempt to find the perfect make-up for my skin. In hindsight, however, what I really should have done was to organize to have a make-up artist come directly to my home instead.

And as a result of the different make-up artists having applied the same make-up on me as they had used with other females at the shopping centre, I contracted glandular fever.

I was so ill during this time, including the three weeks leading up to my wedding, that it placed a real damper on my wedding preparations, and I had never been as ill from a virus, long-term, as I was from this particular strain.

I constantly felt so exhausted, and continually needed to rest. I believed that I was so unlucky at the time because my glandular fever was preventing me from fully enjoying what was meant to be one of the happiest times of my life. And when my wedding day finally arrived, I was extremely happy but really tired and unwell from the glandular fever simultaneously.

Penelope was the maid of honour at my wedding. One of Sam's sisters was my bridesmaid. I wore a white bridal gown with a long train, laced with the most beautiful beads, which was simply exquisite!

The Church ceremony was really beautiful, and I was so happy and proud at having married my soulmate, and the best husband in the world. However, the wedding car broke down whilst we were in the midst of taking our wedding photos which delayed proceedings somewhat, but we still managed to arrive at our reception on time. We then went on to enjoy our honeymoon together at a lovely beach location interstate.

Sadly, however, we were unable to engage in much sightseeing on our honeymoon due to my glandular fever, and my constant feeling of exhaustion. But we still managed to enjoy each other's company nevertheless.

And to make matters worse, my husband contracted gout from eating too many 'trigger foods' at the buffets that were included with our accommodation. My husband never drank alcohol which is said to be a trigger for gout, but he had genetically inherited this medical condition from his father who was also a gout sufferer. I had figured that we were practising our wedding vows whereby the priest states that a couple support each other, 'both in sickness and in health', much earlier than I had anticipated!

For the first two years of our marriage, Sam and I travelled as much as we possibly could. We had decided to put on hold starting a family until we had seen more of the world. We travelled throughout Australia and to countries like New Zealand, the USA and Europe as a married couple. We always had such a wonderful time travelling together. I absolutely loved being with my husband for every minute of every day, and I never tired of his company.

But then, once we no longer felt the desire to travel anymore, we decided that it was time to start a family. I was now thirty-two years of age. But as the months turned into years, I had still not fallen pregnant, as yet. Anxiety began to take hold of me. Was there something wrong with either of us? I just couldn't understand why it was taking so long. Was this normal? We made an appointment to see my gynaecologist who suggested that we both undergo some tests to find out exactly why I was experiencing difficulty in becoming pregnant.

Tests did, in fact, reveal that there was a physical problem involved which was preventing me from getting pregnant. My gynaecologist discussed the possibility of seeking the help of a fertility clinic. I was devastated and in great shock, as I never expected this to happen to me.

For most of my life, all I had ever wanted was to get married and have children. And now, I was unable to become pregnant. I was faced with the harsh reality that I may actually remain childless forever. I may never be blessed with the family that I had desperately craved for so many years. I honestly felt as though my entire world was falling apart around me.

I was not ambitious. I desperately wanted to be a mother and have many children. After all, I had become a primary school teacher because I loved children, and really enjoyed their company. I had just assumed that I would be able to become pregnant easily, and have as many children as I desired. I never thought, in my wildest dreams, that I wouldn't even be able to have one child, let alone have many children.

And during this most devastating time for me, I continued to work at the women's hospital. I would see pregnant women walking around the hospital constantly, and I was so envious of them. I remember seeing a pregnant lady smoking whilst entering a lift and I couldn't help but wonder to myself, why has God blessed this woman with a child when she is putting her own baby's health at risk by smoking whilst being pregnant?

After discussing our situation and dilemma at great length, Sam and I decided not to go ahead with seeking assistance from the fertility clinic. It just wasn't the way my husband and I had envisaged that I would become pregnant. After searching my soul, I slowly began to realize that maybe I just wasn't meant to get pregnant; maybe I wasn't meant to become a mother, and maybe it was God's Will that we were to never experience parenthood.

And during this most distressing time, I also arrived at the strong realization that God had blessed me with, and introduced into my life, the best and most special husband in the entire world. I could never imagine myself being as happy and content with anyone else, no matter how much money or wealth they possessed nor what position they held in life. Sam was my soulmate; I was deeply in love with him, and I knew that there would never be another man in my life who could ever take his place. So finally, I learnt to accept my fate, and I gave up on my dream of ever becoming a mother.

Sam lived an extremely busy life – by night, he studied part-time and was undertaking an IT degree by distance education. In his spare time, he was engaged in writing a software program for Penelope, free of charge. And by day, he worked full-time for an IT company. So, in essence, my husband had very little time to actually spend with me during the day or night.

On the other hand, I always experienced great boredom once I had completed all of my daily chores; I had nothing to do at night-time really, except watch some television which I did by myself in the bedroom until bedtime, waiting for the night to be over and for the next day to come.

One evening, after dinner, I was particularly bored whilst Sam was working on some assignments for his university course. So, I turned on my computer, and came across the Catholic Online website. There, I read an account about St Bernadette and Our Lady who had appeared to this Saint in several apparitions at Lourdes in France.

I was absolutely fascinated by these apparitions, and I later mentioned this to my husband. And at the time, I remember saying to him earnestly, "If only I had some Holy Water from Lourdes, I know that I could get pregnant." And most surprisingly, Sam said that his grandmother had visited Lourdes before she had passed away and had brought back some Holy Water in a coke bottle, which was now thirty years old, and was in the possession of Sam's mother.

Soon after, Sam's mother gave me a tiny bottle filled with a very small amount of genuine Holy Water from Lourdes. I was almost too afraid to touch the water, because it was so Holy and I felt most unworthy at the time. But eventually, I dipped my finger into the Holy Water and making the sign of the Cross on my stomach, I prayed to Our Lady to be able to get pregnant, and become a mother.

And the very next month, I fell pregnant with my daughter, Therese. I was thirty-five years of age. And when it was time for my first ultrasound at twelve weeks, my risk of having a down syndrome baby was assessed as being one in ten thousand. They told me that it was like I was a fifteen-year-old teenager having a baby. I knew that this baby was a true miracle and a special gift from the Mother of God, and that Therese would be a very special person when she grew up.

I experienced morning sickness for eight months of my pregnancy. I actually lost some weight whilst being pregnant because I felt so nauseous all the time, and I struggled to eat. But I didn't care. I was just so grateful for being able to finally become pregnant. It was a most exciting time for Sam and I.

And when my due date arrived, I did not go into labour, however. As each day passed, nothing happened. My baby was refusing to come out! Maybe she was too comfortable in my womb, and was not yet ready to face the world! But after being six days overdue, my obstetrician decided to induce me, and I finally went into labour. The labour pains were so great that I opted for an epidural which immediately eliminated the pain, and I actually fell asleep for a while. I experienced a six-and-a-half-hour labour in total, and I woke up, just in time, when my baby was ready to enter the world.

After the successful birth of my daughter, I was haemorrhaging and it took a while for the obstetrician to stop the bleeding. I received many stitches, as a result, and experienced an enormous amount of pain afterwards. But I didn't care because becoming a mother, and having a baby daughter, was one of the greatest and most special gifts that God could have ever bestowed upon me.

I spent five days in hospital with my daughter and husband. I really struggled to breastfeed Therese but I was determined to do so, and I never gave up until I had mastered this skill. I had always imagined breastfeeding to be so easy and to come naturally to me, but I was most surprised when I experienced neither of these scenarios.

Whilst still in hospital, a really sweet Catholic Nun entered my room, since I was a patient in a Catholic private hospital. She sat down in my room, and we had a lovely chat together. I told her all about the Holy Water from Lourdes, and how the miracle of my daughter had occurred as a result of my faith and the power of the Holy Water. She just sat there listening intently to my story and once I had finished, she asked me a question, most solemnly, which absolutely shocked me. She said, "Do you know what my name is?" I shook my head in response, and told her that I did not. She then immediately replied, "My name is Sr Bernadette Mary." I was most stunned the moment she told me her name. I strongly felt that this was beyond just being a coincidence. Sr Bernadette Mary then proceeded to tell me that, one day, I should visit Lourdes with my daughter. And this has actually been one of my dreams in life which I really hope will become reality, one day, in the near future.

## CHAPTER 7

After my daughter was born, I became extremely close to Our Lady, the Mother of God, since I was so incredibly grateful to Her for having answered my prayers. My faith in Our Lady, and in God, grew from strength to strength, and it was a really happy time for me, until my next challenging trial eventuated.

When my daughter was only nine months old, I found a breast lump. I was terrified and during the ultrasound, the radiologist was called in afterwards. He said that the lump was causing a shadow and when I asked him what this meant, he replied that cancer usually causes a shadow to appear in the image. Immediately, my heart sank and I was in the pits of despair. I had never been so frightened in my entire life as I was during this time, and all I could think about was my baby daughter who was still so young and needed me to look after her.

After undergoing a breast biopsy, I was so relieved and grateful to God when I received my results. The lump was, in fact, benign and was found to be only a breastfeeding lump.

I was always so grateful to God and Our Lady for having allowed me to experience the immense joys of motherhood, and for giving me the most special Christmas present that I could ever have asked for or received in my life. I felt truly blessed to be a mother.

And in my extreme gratitude to God for having allowed me to have a child, I didn't dare pray for another. Therese was a true miracle from God, and I honestly felt as though it would be most selfish of me to pray for another child or expect to become pregnant, once more.

But after almost four years had passed, another miracle occurred in my life when I most unexpectedly, fell pregnant with my second child, a son. This pregnancy was not as difficult as my first. Although I felt nauseous on most mornings, I never actually vomited. And my son, Michael, was much more active in the womb than was my daughter. He would kick me with such strength that it honestly felt as though he was doing somersaults in my womb! It was a most joyous time for Sam and I and we couldn't wait to meet our son when he was due to be born.

My obstetrician had advised me not to have an epidural this time, after reassuring me that my labour would most likely be much shorter than my first and according to his prediction, I would experience an easy birth in general. But how wrong could he have been!

Just as my son was about to enter the world, my obstetrician noticed that the umbilical cord was loosely wrapped twice around his neck and so he performed an urgent episiotomy, even before the local anaesthetic that he had injected had had a chance to take effect. But I ignored the pain because I was most concerned about my baby, and I just wanted him to be born safe and sound. Again, I haemorrhaged after my son's birth, just as I had with my daughter, and I received many stitches, as a result.

A few hours later, however, whilst already in my hospital ward,

I became concerned when I realized that I was still bleeding considerably, and the haemorrhaging had not stopped, as yet. So, I had to endure another round of stitches which consequently stopped the blood loss but caused more excruciating pain for me than I was already experiencing at the time. Fortunately, I was given strong pain killers to take which helped ease the pain somewhat. But since I was breastfeeding my son, I was reluctant to take too many painkillers, and so my pain and suffering became more intense at times.

On the day after my son's birth, I felt a considerably sharp but constant pain in my calf. My obstetrician immediately diagnosed me with superficial thrombosis. So, once I left the hospital (I only stayed two nights because I wanted to go home to be with Therese, as well), Sam injected Clexane into my stomach for ten days afterwards to dissolve the blood clot that had developed in my calf.

One night, Michael woke up, screaming. I picked him up, out of his cot, and cuddled him. But since he wouldn't stop crying, I sat down in a chair in our bedroom, and breastfed him for a while instead. I was so tired that I must have fallen asleep for a brief moment whilst breastfeeding Michael. And at this point in time, I suddenly saw a crystal clear vision of St Mary MacKillop. It was as though I was looking at a photo of her. I just knew that it was Australia's first and only Saint, and so I began to pray to her afterwards. This vision actually occurred during the time of St Mary MacKillop's canonization. After this vision had disappeared, I suddenly awoke feeling most surprised that I had seen St Mary MacKillop so clearly in my vision, amidst the dark surroundings of my bedroom. And although I didn't understand why I had had the vision of this wonderful Saint, I really didn't think anything of it since I had grown quite accustomed to experiencing supernatural occurrences in my life. Consequently, I continued to breastfeed Michael until he fell asleep again.

Michael suffered from extreme colic for the first eight months of his life. He would wake up often during the night, screaming, and sometimes he would even get into the habit of waking up every fifteen minutes or so, and I would breastfeed him each and every time he awoke in an attempt to settle him, as quickly as possible. But he continued to be a very poor sleeper, even as he grew older. He would wake up crying, multiple times during the night, and I would consistently breastfeed him every single time until he would fall asleep again.

In desperation, Sam and I took Michael to see a number of different paediatricians who all said the same thing. He was a healthy and alert baby who would grow out of his poor sleep patterns by the age of three. And they were right!

One afternoon, whilst Sam was working in our backyard, he had a terrible accident. At the time we had bought our property, there was a large wooden frame in our backyard that was attached to the fence bordering our neighbour's property. It was an eyesore and as a result, my husband had decided to remove this frame all by himself. It was an enormous frame and quite heavy, much heavier than Sam had anticipated, I believe.

I was actually upstairs at the time, and I had no idea of the awful and most unexpected incident that was currently taking place, involving Sam, in our backyard.

I stared at my husband in surprise when he suddenly appeared before me. Sam was just standing there, holding his wrist outwards and said, in such a calm voice, "I think I have broken my wrist." With my mouth open in shock, I looked down at his wrist and screamed in panic since the bone had visibly come out of alignment. And my husband had also sustained a bleeding wound on his forehead, as well. Sam had underestimated the weight of the large wooden frame which had accidentally fallen on top of him.

Sam went to hospital and required an operation. He finally had the operation on his wrist at around 2.30 am in the morning which had also consisted of implanting a number of screws and plates to assist in the healing process. He was discharged from hospital later that day.

Sam had broken his wrist just three weeks before Christmas. Having his arm in a sling and not being able to use one hand was difficult for Sam, and made celebrating Christmas more challenging. But we still managed to have a lovely Christmas, despite the hurdle that Sam and our entire family had had to overcome during this time.

By the time Michael was eight months old, I had already lost 20 kg. I was absolutely exhausted. The sleep deprivation that I experienced as a result of Michael's constant bouts of colic was taking a toll on my health. My obstetrician was most concerned about my extreme weight loss, and ordered a series of blood tests which showed that I was very low in vitamin D. He recommended that I take supplements for my deficiency. However, since I was breastfeeding Michael at the time, I was concerned about the impact that taking vitamin supplements may ultimately have on my son. So, in the end, I failed to take any supplements for my vitamin D deficiency, much to my own detriment.

I was constantly so exhausted that I could barely eat. I even struggled to swallow food. I was just never hungry anymore. I found that I was suffering from extreme fatigue on a continual basis.

Then when Michael was about three years of age, and my daughter was in Grade 1 at primary school, my life suddenly took a turn for the worse as my health unexpectedly deteriorated most rapidly. I found myself going on a downwards spiral and my life, as I knew it, was completely and utterly turned upside down in what seemed like only a split second.

# CHAPTER 8

It was summertime, and we were all enjoying the Christmas break. My daughter had suddenly come down with a form of gastroenteritis in which she didn't actually vomit but every time Therese ate something, her stomach would hurt and she would have to lie down and rest for a while. She also experienced extreme tiredness at the time from this particular virus. After Therese had recovered, I contracted the same illness, and I recovered fully within about a week.

About two days after I had recovered from the stomach virus, my entire family and I decided to go shopping in a nearby supermarket. As I was walking around the store, I noticed that my toes suddenly felt very odd. I didn't know how to describe the feeling because I had never experienced this sensation before. But I tried to ignore it, and I hoped that this strange feeling in my toes would just go away on its own.

But it didn't go away; it only grew worse. The next morning, when I awoke and rose out of bed, the back of my calves felt numb. And as each day passed, the numbness continued to travel up my body until it had progressed to the back of my thighs, waist and fingers. I was, by now, in a real state of panic. I didn't know what was happening to me. I failed to know when this horrific ordeal would end, or if the numbness would actually stop travelling through my body parts. I had no idea what was wrong with me. And there are no words to describe how distressed and terrified I was at the time.

I consulted with a general physician who was just as baffled as I was by my sudden onset of experiencing numbness in my body. She had absolutely no idea what was wrong with me and she recommended that I undertake a full body MRI (Magnetic Resonance Imaging), as a result.

I will never forget the day that my physician rang me at home with the results. She began our conversation by informing me that she had received the results for my MRI, and she had strongly emphasized that they were abnormal. At hearing this frightening news, my heart sank and I dreaded hearing anymore. And what made matters even worse, were the questions that she asked me immediately afterwards. She said, "Are you sitting down? Is your husband there with you? Can you call him?" I was beside myself with terror at the way that she was reacting.

My physician then proceeded to tell me that the MRI had showed that I had six white spots in my neck and spine, and that I probably had MS (Multiple Sclerosis). And then most casually she said that it was okay because I may only ever have one episode in my life.

I asked her if I would end up in a wheelchair, and she said that I most likely would not. My physician recommended that I consult with a female neurologist that she knew which I did as soon as I was able to get an appointment with her.

At my initial consultation with the neurologist, she immediately asked me if I had recently received the vaccine for cervical cancer because she had consulted with a patient whose 'spine lit up like a Christmas tree', on her MRI results, directly after receiving this vaccine. I had not, however, ever received this vaccine.

The neurologist wanted me to have an MRI with contrast at 3 weeks, 6 weeks, 3 months and at 6 months. I felt as though I was a guinea pig in an experiment. So, my sibling, who actually worked in the medical field, found another neurologist for me whose expertise was specifically in MS. It was his bread and butter, and I was most impressed with him at my initial consultation.

I asked my new neurologist if he believed that I actually had MS since the mere thought of having this disease terrified me more than I can express in words. He said that I currently did not have MS because MS actually stands for Multiple Sclerosis, and I had experienced only one episode of demyelination in my neck and spine to date. Fortunately, it had not occurred in my brain.

But then, he proceeded to tell me that if I were to receive any further lesions, however, I would be diagnosed with MS. There are no words that could describe how I felt at this moment. I was experiencing a mixture of fear, extreme anxiety, melancholy, depression, disillusionment and desperation, to say the least. I found myself hoping against hope that I would not get any more lesions because in my heart I knew that emotionally, I would not be able to handle being told that I had MS.

After asking my neurologist what the treatment for MS entailed, I found that he was rather reluctant to discuss this in much detail with me. But he did briefly mention that it would involve weekly or monthly injections. My neurologist basically did not wish to discuss this matter any further unless deemed necessary in the future.

During our consultation, I asked the neurologist to explain exactly what had happened to me, as I didn't quite understand much about my newly diagnosed condition. He then proceeded to tell me that whilst my immune system was fighting off the stomach virus that I had recently contracted, my T-cells had actually gone into overdrive to destroy the virus and had simultaneously attacked the nerve coating on some of the nerves in my neck and spine - hence, the numbness I experienced, as a result.

The neurologist had also informed me that sometimes the nerve coating can grow back and regenerate but in other cases, it cannot. And the estimated time frame for recovery was about two years if the nerve coating was able to regenerate, that is, which was the best-case scenario. So, I had absolutely no way of knowing if I would ever be able to recover from my illness; only time would tell.

At the end of the consultation, the neurologist had recommended that I have an MRI in six months' time, just to see whether I had any new lesions. If they happened to discover any new lesions in my MRI in the near future, however, then I would immediately be diagnosed with having MS.

I went home feeling depressed and disheartened. My biggest fear in life at the time was if I would be diagnosed with MS at some time in the future. I was told not to do any spring cleaning at home, and to have plenty of rest. There was no other treatment that I was given for my numbness and as this advice had been strongly recommended, I strictly adhered to it.

One of the most difficult things that I had to deal with during this time of great suffering was that I felt totally useless both as a wife and mother. I remember standing in the kitchen whilst attempting to hand wash some of the dishes that were soaking in the sink. But the plates kept slipping out of my hands, and I kept dropping things onto the floor because my fingers felt so numb that I was now unable to grip objects properly. So, my husband sent me out of the kitchen to rest, and I just sat down on the couch in the loungeroom and watched my children play.

I quickly realized that I was now incapable of undertaking the usual chores that I had previously taken for granted in the past. I struggled to brush my teeth at night; hold a pen in my hand to sign my signature; as well as tie my young daughter's hair in a ponytail each morning before school. And with fingers as numb as mine were at the time, tying Therese's hair back, for example, was an almost impossible feat but I failed to give up until I had succeeded in overcoming each and every one of my new daily challenges. And when drying my daughter's hair with a hair dryer, I couldn't even feel if her hair was wet or dry, so I would have to ask Therese to touch her head and let me know when her hair felt dry.

I felt so incredibly guilty because my husband now had to do practically everything by himself. I experienced intense feelings of uselessness and great remorse. My husband was working full-time, cooking, doing the housework and looking after two young children, practically on his own and all I could do, most of the time, was to just sit around and rest.

But Sam never complained to me, not even once, about the enormous burden that had, suddenly and most unexpectedly, been placed upon his shoulders, and he efficiently and diligently continued to run our household with barely any help from me at all.

Walking my daughter to the nearby primary school each morning was an arduous task in itself because we were often late to school, since I struggled to complete the necessary tasks that I was previously able to achieve effortlessly before school in the past.

One morning, Therese and I bumped into the school principal who saw us arriving late which was as a result of my newly diagnosed medical condition. She basically reprimanded me for bringing Therese late to school. Although I apologized to her, I did not explain my situation to the principal and go into detail as to why we were often so late. Emotionally, I just couldn't talk about my numbness with others. If I were to reflect on my condition, I would feel as though I was experiencing numbness to an even greater degree. I was emotionally and psychologically distraught about my numbness. I hid my intense suffering from other people, and I had even tried my utmost to hide it from my own children. I had reasoned that what was the point of them knowing the truth and in being upset about it? I just wanted my children to be happy, and not to have to worry about me.

Privately, however, I would break down and cry to my husband about my numbness symptoms, and discuss my condition with him. Sam was always so incredibly supportive and positive. He would never allow me to become negative or to indulge in self-pity. Sam was my rock at the time, and I honestly don't know what I would have done without him, and his constant and unfailing support.

He continually believed that I would recover from my illness. Sam was truly the best, most supportive and loyal husband in the entire world.

During my illness, I could always walk but, unbeknown to me at the time, I could not run. And this fact could not have been highlighted any more than during a most frightening incident that occurred on one occasion, which I will never forget for as long as I live.

One day, whilst holding onto my three-year-old's hand as we were walking to school at pick-up time, Michael suddenly let go of my hand and began to race down the street towards the road. I was terrified that Michael may get run over if he chose to cross the road at the intersection, so I began to chase after him. But to my shock and dismay, just as I began to run, my entire body suddenly jolted abruptly, and it was at this moment that I realized that I had lost the ability to run. My heart sank and I began to panic, more than words can ever hope to express. And even to this day, a number of years later, I can still remember my entire body jolting, most suddenly and severely, before coming to a sudden halt, as I tried to run to save my son. It was the eeriest, strangest and most scary feeling that I have ever encountered before.

Fortunately for Michael, Sam was following closely behind me. And racing down the footpath, ahead of me, my husband grabbed our son, just in time, before he ran across the road. From that point onwards, I was terrified to be left alone with my son because I felt so inadequate as a mother due to my inability to be able to run in an emergency, and to my numbness in general which was quickly proving to be completely and utterly ruining my life, in every way possible.

But the aspect that upset me the most, during this extraordinarily difficult time of great suffering, was the numbness that I was experiencing in my waist. Basically, my waist felt as though I was wearing a tight belt around it constantly, and it didn't matter if I was lying, sitting or standing, I could never get any relief from this sensation of great tightness. But what I feared the most, however, was that my waist would remain numb forever. I honestly didn't know how I could continue to live my life like this, long-term, or worse still, on a permanent basis. Sometimes, I even felt as though I was struggling to breathe, and I would often have to inhale deeply to get more air into my lungs. Furthermore, I experienced panic attacks since I was terrified that the numbness would affect my lungs in due course, and that I would end up being unable to breathe or in a wheelchair, for that matter.

However, I did not allow myself the luxury of wallowing in self-pity and I tried my utmost, to always remain in a relatively positive frame of mind. I just knew that I simply had to live my life as best as I could under the new and current circumstances.

But then, I suddenly realized that I actually had two choices in life: I could either take the easy path - just give up and resign myself to experiencing the numbness forever, or I could fight back and try my utmost to recover from this debilitating illness. I chose the latter.

# CHAPTER 9

During my illness, I would experience both good and bad days. On the good days, I would become much more optimistic since I felt as though I was actually making progress in regaining some feeling back. But then, the very next day, I would experience extreme disappointment when the numbness would completely return to its former self. And during these times, I really felt as though I was back to square one again. The enormous mountain which had, suddenly and most unexpectedly, appeared in my path, seemed insurmountable to me, at first, and I had no idea if I would ever be able to reach the top and be victorious.

Nevertheless, I began the arduous task of climbing up this mountain which seemed to almost touch the sky. But when I reached halfway, and had recovered some feeling in the back of my calves and thighs, my numbness would suddenly return and I could feel myself slipping further and further down the mountain until I had reached rock bottom. I immediately rang my neurologist and told him about my good and bad days, and he said that this was, in fact, the nature of my illness which I found most reassuring to hear at the time.

After six months had passed, I couldn't bring myself to have the MRI that my neurologist had recommended. I was terrified that more lesions would be found, and I would be diagnosed with MS. Although I had regained the feeling in my legs, my waist and fingers were still very numb. At this stage in my life, I knew, deep down, that I just wouldn't be able to emotionally handle being told that I had MS. And since I was slowly but surely recovering, I decided to hold off on having the MRI for the time being anyway.

Positive thinking was crucial in my recovery. After about a year had passed, my fingers and waist were still numb and had not improved. I decided that I really needed to know whether or not I had MS for my own peace of mind. I was now ready to take the plunge, and discover the truth about my current illness. And after mustering up the courage to have the MRI, I was most relieved when my results remained unchanged. At this stage, I still did not have MS. I was so grateful to God, and I became even more optimistic and determined to recover fully from my illness.

But I was still extremely upset about the tightness sensation that I was experiencing in my waist, and the fact that I often felt as though I was struggling to breathe. I just felt so uncomfortable all the time.

One morning, I decided to attend a school Mass with my daughter. After Mass, the Parish Priest was standing outside the Church, greeting the children and parents who had attended. I went over to him and told the priest about my numbness condition, and particularly about the numbness in my waist which was distressing me the most. He was greatly sympathetic, and told me that he would pray for me. I was extremely appreciative, and I felt so much happier after our brief discussion. And I can genuinely say that within the next two days, the numbness in my waist was no more, and the feeling suddenly returned.

I had assumed that God had answered the prayers of this Catholic parish priest and for some reason, I had possessed tremendous faith in this particular priest whom I had always deemed to be most Holy.

I was so grateful to God for having allowed me to regain feeling in my waist again. I honestly felt as though I would be able to tolerate my suffering if the numbness were to remain permanently in my fingers. But I had been struggling to deal with the numbness in my waist immensely ever since it occurred, and more than words can ever hope to express. It was a tremendous feeling to be able to breathe properly again, and without having to experience such laboured breathing all the time.

After two years, I had another full body MRI and the results showed that two of the lesions had, in fact, disappeared. I immediately knew that these lesions must have been the ones that were causing the numbness in my waist, and I was so encouraged by the fact that I only had four lesions left now.

Although I was still so grateful to God for having regained the feeling in my waist, I continued to pray to Him to be able to make a full recovery from my illness. After three long and arduous years had passed, however, and as a result of my constant prayers to God, my husband's tremendous and continual support, my positive thinking and enormous drive to defeat this illness, I recovered almost fully from my numbness.

I felt so proud of myself, and I experienced such an enormous sense of achievement for having continued to climb this gigantic mountain that had suddenly appeared before me, seemingly out of nowhere, and for having never given up despite encountering so many setbacks, as well as in being victorious at reaching the very top of this mountain, at last.

At this point in time, I also undertook my final full body MRI. The results showed that my four remaining lesions had become so small that they were barely visible. And my neurologist had told me that I no longer needed to see him anymore since I had, more or less, recovered from my illness.

At having regained all feeling in my fingers, I was so grateful to God for having recovered, almost completely, from my illness that I really wanted to make a positive contribution to society in return. So, I decided to become a children's author, and I wrote my first novel about bullying and its consequences.

Within four years, I had already written and published a number of children's books. I was extremely proud of each and every one of them. I truly loved them all, and I was most passionate about the importance of reading books.

But once my collection of children's books was complete, I began the arduous task of advertising my books through social media. After a short period of time, I had managed to sell a few copies of each of my books, but nowhere near enough for my liking. At this point in time, I was beginning to realize just how difficult the marketing side of my business was proving to be. Initially, however, I had been so naïve in thinking that my books would actually have the ability to sell themselves! But how wrong could I have been!

I had specifically written an exciting and educational collection of children's books, each of which contained the most beautiful and vibrant coloured illustrations, in an attempt to entice children to wish to read the books. But as I soon found out later, having a unique range of most engaging children's books was just not enough. I had to learn how to market my books effectively which is something that I was totally unprepared for and that I feared the most.

I had never considered myself to be a good salesperson. I lacked self-confidence, I had an extremely low self-esteem, and I possessed a very negative attitude in life.

Consequently, I was now faced with the dilemma of having published a collection of the most beautiful children's books but not being able to market them effectively due to my extreme lack of self-confidence, and the fact that I didn't have the courage to talk to strangers to discuss the merits of my books in an attempt to encourage book sales.

During this time, I had generated a number of social media accounts, and had accumulated more than a thousand followers and connections for each of these platforms. Although I had sold only a small quantity of my books through social media, I had actually made a few really nice friends as a result of using social media. I would often upload posts about my books, and receive such lovely feedback from my followers, as well as from other users.

By now, however, I had already formed the opinion that I was not intelligent or good enough to be able to ever become a successful children's author. I was now beginning to feel that I had, in essence, wasted years of my life, time and money in producing and publishing a collection of children's books which I just couldn't sell due to my extreme lack of self-confidence and low self-esteem.

And at this point, I was more upset about being a failure than words can ever hope to be able to express.

# CHAPTER 10

When my son was in his first year at primary school, he started coughing and developed a fever. Sam and I took him to our local doctor who prescribed Michael with some antibiotics. But his cough became even worse over the next few days, and we ended up having to take Michael to see a paediatrician who diagnosed him with atypical pneumonia. The paediatrician prescribed Michael with a course of strong antibiotics.

It was a rather difficult time for all members of our household. At night, in particular, I could hear my son's chest crackling as a result of the pneumonia when he breathed. It was a most frightening experience to have to endure and Michael's fever remained for nine consecutive days. He also missed school due to his illness.

Michael was prescribed another course of strong antibiotics once he had completed his first course since his pneumonia was not yet fully resolved. But I was just so grateful and relieved that Michael could be treated at home rather than having to be admitted to hospital, and that he was slowly but surely recovering from his illness.

I constantly prayed to God for our son to make a complete and speedy recovery from his pneumonia and over time, Michael did, in fact, recover fully from his illness, and our lives were able to resume some sort of normality, once again.

But this period of time was only short-lived, however. Before long, my emotions were taken for a ride on a roller coaster again when I was confronted with another most difficult and frightening obstacle that had suddenly appeared in my path, seemingly out of nowhere.

Soon after Michael had recovered from his illness, I had to undergo another difficult trial in my life and one which I will never forget; it was the day that I discovered another breast lump. And as soon as I had found this lump, I was terrified because the lump felt quite hard although it did seem to move around a little when pressed. My doctor immediately ordered an ultrasound which showed that the lump, in fact, consisted of a solid as well as a fluid component. So, I was forced to undergo my second breast biopsy which again, was a most frightening ordeal.

The laboratory results showed that the breast lump was most likely a papilloma. Now, there are two types of papillomas – one is precancerous, and the other type is benign. My surgeon had no way of knowing exactly which type of papilloma my breast lump had embodied, and so I underwent surgery to excise the lump.

I cannot express in words how terrified I felt whilst waiting for the laboratory analysis to be conducted of the breast lump. And when my breast surgeon finally called me with the results, I could feel my heart pounding in great anticipation and terror of the news that she was about to relay. I was so anxious at the time that I could barely focus on the words that she was imparting. But when she told me that the breast lump was benign, I was overshadowed with an enormous sense of relief and pure joy. I was so grateful to God that my breast lump was not cancerous, and that it was benign, after all.

After having recovered from my breast surgery, I realized that I had now actually become afraid of being happy in life. Every time I experienced happiness, something really bad would happen in my life simultaneously, and my happiness would become extremely short-lived.

So, in essence, from thereon, I lived my life being too afraid to be really happy again. I always waited in anticipation for the next really bad event to occur in my life and before long, it did actually eventuate. But I had no idea that the situation that was about to unfold would cause me to experience so much angst and emotional torture, that I simply did not know how I would ever be able to get through it successfully.

Therese was in Grade 5 at primary school at the time. She had come home from school, one day, and in passing conversation had mentioned that she was experiencing some pain in her right thigh. I asked Therese what she had done at school that day, since she had participated in a physical education class. My daughter informed me that the school had run a cricket clinic and I quickly dismissed her pain as being just muscle pain in her leg, as a result.

But over the next few days, her pain had not resolved. I began to feel slightly anxious as a consequence which resulted in Sam and I deciding to take Therese to consult with a paediatrician. After his initial examination, the paediatrician remarked that her pain could be from the early onset of SUFE (Slipped Upper Femoral Epiphysis) but he didn't believe this to be the case. The paediatrician recommended that she refrain from participating in any sporting activities for the time being, and to monitor her pain.

But the pain never went away. One day, whilst Therese was sitting on the loungeroom floor with her brother and cousin, my daughter suddenly decided to get up, for some unknown reason, and walk towards the kitchen which was only a short distance away. And I was most alarmed when I immediately noticed that Therese was swinging her right leg out without even realizing that she was doing so. My sibling, who was visiting us at the time, was also extremely perturbed, informing us simultaneously that we needed to take Therese to see an orthopaedic specialist immediately.

We soon found an orthopaedic surgeon who worked in the area and after careful examination, he immediately said, with great conviction, that Therese had developed SUFE – a condition whereby the ball in the hip had started to slip out of the growth plate.

An x-ray confirmed his diagnosis. SUFE is an extremely serious condition which is termed an orthopaedic emergency, and requires immediate surgery.

The orthopaedic specialist that Sam and I had found ourselves had not performed many of this type of surgery before and so, my sibling found another surgeon who was far more experienced in this area since it was, in fact, his bread and butter.

We consulted with the new surgeon on a Friday, and booked Therese for surgery on the following Monday. Although our daughter's surgery was elective, it was urgent. The orthopaedic surgeon emphasized how important it was for Therese not to engage in any form of physical activity including walking, over the weekend. He also advised us to obtain a wheelchair, as well as some crutches, and to disallow Therese to bear any weight whatsoever on her right leg as this could cause the ball in her hip to slip even further out of the growth plate.

He then proceeded to tell us a story about another little girl who was about the same age as Therese, and was a past patient of the orthopaedic surgeon. She had presented to him on a Friday, just like Therese, and her surgery had been scheduled to take place on the following Monday. But sadly, and most unfortunately, this particular little girl had fallen over in the bathroom over the weekend and her diagnosis had been altered from being Stage 1 to Stage 3 for SUFE. She had ended up requiring a hip replacement at the age of only ten, as a result.

After hearing this story, I was terrified for Therese's welfare. So, Sam and I were extremely careful over the weekend so as not to allow our daughter to bear any weight on her right leg whatsoever to avoid a similar situation from occurring with Therese.

When Monday arrived, our daughter underwent surgery and the orthopaedic surgeon implanted a large screw in her right hip. The surgery went well, and I stayed with her overnight in hospital. Therese received strong painkillers during her hospital stay, and slept most of the time.

She was discharged from hospital the following morning. When Therese arrived home, she was now wheelchair bound. The surgeon had watched Therese using crutches before the surgery and as she didn't appear to be stable enough, he felt that it was too big a risk for Therese to use them solely for mobility. So, he strongly recommended and advised that she always sit in a wheelchair, for six weeks in total, and to use the crutches only minimally and when absolutely necessary.

Upon waking up, after spending her first night at home from hospital, Therese turned to look at me. The expression on her face was that of great melancholy and depression, and it absolutely broke my heart to see my daughter react in this way which was totally out of character for her.

It was more than obvious to me that Therese was really struggling with her emotions, and that she was courageously trying her utmost to hold back the tears. And then, she absolutely broke my heart, even more, when she said, "Mom, what am I going to do for six weeks in a wheelchair?" My heart sank, as I was overshadowed with grief and empathy for my daughter. But I quickly managed to reply, "Well, Therese, you're lucky that you only have to spend six weeks in a wheelchair. Some children have to spend their entire lives in a wheelchair." After I had said this to my daughter, Therese put on a brave face and began her arduous journey of recovery.

Therese did not attend school for the next five weeks. She had actually undertaken her operation during the middle of her school vacation. Although she visited her classmates and teacher once school had resumed, Therese was extremely bored just sitting around in her wheelchair, day in and day out.

Our daughter had been assigned, by her physiotherapist, a number of foot and leg exercises which she needed to perform on a daily basis whilst lying in bed, before she got up. In time, Therese became more and more competent at manoeuvring herself in and out of the wheelchair whilst using her crutches.

All family members had to overcome many challenges during Therese's newly acquired medical condition, especially and including Therese. Having showers and manoeuvring the wheelchair into the bathroom was tricky, because our house had not been designed for wheelchair access.

We were told, by the surgeon, that it was of vital importance that Therese did not bear any weight on her right leg whatsoever for the first six weeks after her surgery. And so, Therese learnt very quickly to use only her left leg whilst manoeuvring herself in and out of the wheelchair. We were also told that if she did happen to bear any weight on her right leg, then the ball in her hip could actually continue to slip, and that this would warrant further surgery in which case another screw would have to be inserted into her right hip. We were all definitely not keen for this particular circumstance to eventuate, and so we were continually careful to avoid this scenario from ever coming to fruition.

# CHAPTER 11

Every night, I cried for six weeks as soon as my daughter had gone to bed. I just felt so incredibly melancholy and heartbroken to see Therese stuck in a wheelchair every day from early morning until bedtime at night. It was an enormous burden that I had to carry on my shoulders and in some ways, it was much more difficult to stand by and watch my child suffer personally through a challenging phase in her life than if I had undergone it myself as an adult. It was, in fact, another form of emotional torment and torture which I had no choice but to endure to the best of my ability.

Family outings basically consisted of walking to our local shopping centre whilst pushing Therese around in her wheelchair all the while. Locals would often stare at Therese and smile; it was interesting to note how many looks of sympathy that she actually received from total strangers whilst sitting in a wheelchair. On some occasions, friends would come up to us and give Therese a big hug, and much needed words of support and encouragement which was so greatly appreciated by all of us.

We also continued to attend Church on Sundays and brought Therese along in her wheelchair. The regular parishioners who attended Mass knew us by sight as we were also regulars at the Church.

They would come up to us after Mass and have a chat about Therese's condition, since they were most curious as to why Therese was suddenly wheelchair-bound when they had seen her walking around in Church only recently.

Overall, during the six-week period for which our daughter was stuck in her wheelchair, Therese's brother gave her much needed support and attention all the while, which helped her to be able to cope with her unfortunate circumstances to an even greater degree.

Doctors don't really know exactly what causes SUFE to develop in some children and not in others. Rapid growth is meant to be a risk factor, however, and my daughter grew tall very quickly in a relatively short period of time. At seeing Therese after school, one day, a particular parent once said to me, "Does she ever stop growing?"

The weeks passed and before long, it was time for Therese's six-week check-up and x-ray. Thank God, everything looked fine on the x-ray. And when Therese stood up from her wheelchair, for the first time in six weeks, it was such a beautiful sight just to watch her face visibly light up and glow with happiness as soon as she was allowed to walk around again. Beaming, she mentioned how tall everything looked now and Therese had even appeared to have grown during her time in the wheelchair!

The surgeon then proceeded to carefully explain that Therese was not permitted to play any sport until the screw had served its purpose which was to shut down the growth plate early to prevent the ball in her hip from being able to continue to slip out of the growth plate. Normally, the growth plate shuts down at the age of fourteen, but Therese's was being forced to shut down at the age of only ten.

But although Therese was most grateful for now being allowed to actually walk instead of having to be pushed around continuously in a wheelchair, she still found it quite difficult to always have to remind herself not to run around.

At school, Therese felt quite isolated and very lonely during recess and lunchtime. All of the other children were constantly running around in the playground whilst Therese just sat there by herself, and watched them play. So, taking great pity on his sister, Michael played solely with Therese every day instead, which had the effect of dramatically improving her mood and she became much happier, as a result.

After a period of eight months had lapsed, her growth plate finally shut down. Therese's surgeon was extremely pleased that she had also regained all movement in her right leg which had initially been lost when the ball in her hip had first begun to slip out of the growth plate. I was so grateful to God for Therese's full recovery from her medical condition, and I now felt as though I could truly start to feel happy again.

But my happiness was only short-lived. Another huge and most unexpected setback occurred which, in essence, broke my heart, once more.

Therese was actually due to have the screw removed from her right hip after a period of about one year had passed. But just before the surgery had been scheduled, Therese came downstairs, one morning, and told us that she was now experiencing pain in her left knee. I simply froze in fear, in response, and I found myself being overwhelmed by a sudden feeling of great anxiety and concern. Since the surgeon had informed us, much earlier on, that there was only a ten percent chance that Therese could also develop SUFE in her left hip, I had dismissed this possibility almost totally, as a result.

But nevertheless, we consulted with the orthopaedic surgeon regarding Therese's newfound pain in her left knee. He promptly ordered an x-ray of her left hip which showed that it was normal, and I remember being so incredibly relieved to hear this wonderful news at the time.

The following morning, however, my whole world began to fall apart when Therese came walking down the stairs complaining of pain in her left knee again. Her surgeon immediately wrote a referral for an MRI of her left hip. The results showed that the ball in her hip had, in fact, already begun to slip out of the growth plate, ever so slightly. The slip was so slight, in fact, that a normal x-ray was unable to pick it up.

So, Therese was scheduled for immediate surgery, once again. During the procedure, the surgeon removed the screw from her right hip, and inserted a new screw into her left hip. Again, I stayed with Therese overnight in hospital.

When we arrived home, Therese was deeply depressed, as was I. And I found cheering her up a most difficult task since I was feeling equally as depressed as she was, if not more. I just couldn't believe that Therese was being forced to go through such a traumatic event all over again only this time, I strongly felt that it was even worse than last time because Therese now knew exactly what to expect in the days ahead.

Personally, I piled on thirteen kilograms in weight, as a result of my deep depression; Therese also put on additional weight, especially since the only thing that she found comfort in whilst stuck in her wheelchair was food.

But there was one positive element associated with Therese developing SUFE in her left hip at this particular time. Her growth plate had actually managed to shut down after a period of only three months had passed since she was now closer in age to puberty.

Again, Therese regained full movement in her left leg which had initially been lost at first developing SUFE. The surgeon seemed surprised that Therese had regained full movement in both of her legs after having developed SUFE, and I was just so grateful to God for having allowed my daughter to fully recover from her debilitating illness.

After a period of about a year had passed, when my daughter was in Year 7 at secondary school, Therese underwent surgery to remove the screw in her left hip. My daughter was now free to run around and jump as much as she pleased, without having to worry about the consequences.

But for a number of years afterwards, I couldn't understand why this terrible event had happened to Therese in the first place, and why she had had to endure so much suffering at such a young age.

My daughter would often mention that SUFE had basically robbed her of her childhood, and I could understand exactly what she had meant by this. Hence, I became less and less religious, as a result.

And this was, in essence, the unhappiest time of my life, especially since my faith had wavered so much during this period that I had felt totally lost, which was a most devastating feeling for me to ever have to experience.

It made me think about all of the atheists in this world, and how they must feel every single day of their lives. After all, who can atheists possibly turn to for help in their time of need when something really bad occurs in their life such as developing a devastating illness, for example? Who is able to adequately alleviate and/or eliminate their pain and suffering, especially when modern medicine is unable to help them?

Atheists would have to rely solely on themselves, but since we are nothing without God, I have always imagined that they must feel so helpless, isolated and alone in life, especially during their times of trial and suffering.

On the other hand, I have always retained the belief that if you truly believe that nothing is impossible through God, have faith in God, and possess a strong belief in God Himself, then at least there is always an element of hope, no matter how dire or desperate your situation may seem to be at the time, and miracles can occur since God always has the potential to help us, even when nobody else can. After all, He is the Creator of our world, and there is absolutely nothing that God cannot do. God can and will, answer our prayers. It actually pleases God when we ask Him for His assistance with our day-to-day problems, and He will never abandon us in our time of need.

Shortly after my daughter had recovered fully from SUFE, I

received another big blow which distressed me to no end - my father's Parkinson's disease.

My father had actually developed Parkinson's disease about ten years ago. But he was still living independently at home at this stage. And the problem that he was now being confronted with was that he had recently become prone to falling over, more and more. As a result, my sibling, who took it upon herself to take charge of our father's health, organized for him to consult with a new neurologist. Consequently, he was admitted into a private hospital for the sole purpose of juggling his medications in an attempt to subdue our father's Parkinson's disease in order to prevent him from falling over so frequently.

Upon discharge, my father was admitted to a rehabilitation hospital which was located relatively close to his home. But whilst my father was a patient at this rehabilitation hospital, the unthinkable happened - he was accidentally overdosed on Parkinson's medications. A young doctor, who was on duty at the time, misread his medical chart, overdosing him simultaneously, and the end result was that my father was actually given nine tablets instead of the usual four to take which immediately had a most detrimental effect on his health. As a consequence, my father was unable to talk for a period of time until the side effects of the tablets gradually wore off. But the overdose seemed to have a permanent detrimental effect on his health, however.

Parkinson's medications can exhibit really bad side effects in patients who are on these medications. A neurologist told Penelope that the overdose had most likely accelerated our father's Parkinson's disease and as a consequence of the overdose, he had to be admitted to an aged care facility once discharged from the rehabilitation hospital. Our father had lost his independence as a result of the medical mishap which had ruined his quality of life, most likely accelerated our father's Parkinson's disease and caused so much grief, angst and unhappiness for my entire family.

And as a result of the occurrence of this medical mishap, the rehabilitation hospital actually changed their procedures to ensure that this would never happen to another patient again in the future.

# CHAPTER 12

My father was placed in an aged care facility that was relatively close to my home. I visited him on a regular basis but he loathed their food. I must admit that often the food did not look aesthetically appetizing, and I felt sorry for my father and the other residents for being forced to eat this horrible food and having no other choice in the matter. Sam and I often brought my father some home-cooked meals which he devoured immediately and enjoyed very much.

Once, my father had even mentioned to Sam and I that the other residents had also complained about the low quality of the food that was being served to them which caused me to feel extremely sad since I always look forward to my mealtimes and eating foods that are appealing.

Whilst in the aged care facility, my father could walk around with a frame and at this stage, he was still able to walk to the bathroom by himself. He was relatively mobile and independent, and he would often go for short walks up and down the corridors of the aged care facility for exercise.

Being relatively independent at this point in time, my father didn't appear to be miserable living at the aged care facility in which he was a resident. He would frequently listen to his radio or watch television in his room. And whenever my father had to go to the bathroom, he would go by himself without having to summon any staff for help.

My father was always a fiercely independent individual who didn't like having to rely on anyone for help if he could avoid it. But gradually, as his Parkinson's disease worsened, and his health suddenly began to deteriorate quite considerably, it was most difficult to watch him losing his independence before my very eyes, and his deterioration was so obviously becoming more rapid over time.

In the meantime, my mother was experiencing some health problems of her own. She had actually developed heart failure in the past resulting from years of both untreated and uncontrolled high blood pressure when she was younger. My mother's heart was now deteriorating, so much so, that she could only manage to walk a few steps before becoming really puffed resulting in her always having to stop and rest for a while.

Her cardiologist had recommended that she have a pacemaker implanted to improve her heart function and overall quality of life. So, as a result, Penelope as well as my mother and I engaged in an hour-long consultation regarding this procedure with a cardiologist whose great reputation preceded her but who had also come highly recommended to us.

We mainly discussed the possibility of implanting both a defibrillator and a pacemaker, or just a pacemaker on its own. In the end, we decided to implant a pacemaker only which was a much smaller device, and seemed to be the least invasive option. The cardiologist had clearly indicated to us that it was just a routine operation which should take no longer than two-and-a-half hours at the most. She failed to mention any risks associated with this procedure, and as she seemed to possess so much confidence in her abilities, it didn't even enter our minds to ask if there were any complications or risks associated with this type of procedure.

But whilst my mother was undergoing her operation, Penelope and I started to become really concerned after two-and-a-half hours had passed, and yet we had still not received any updates or news regarding the progress of her surgery.

Penelope rang the hospital and spoke to a nurse who informed my sibling that our mother had actually gone into theatre late, but this only slightly reduced our anxiety since a number of hours had already passed and we had still not heard any news regarding the status of our mother's surgery. But after a period of six hours had lapsed, we were told that our mother was finally in recovery in the intensive care unit of the hospital. A combination of shock and extreme angst overshadowed me. A routine pacemaker implant operation which was not expected to have taken longer than two-and-a-half hours in total, had instead lasted for six hours in duration! My mother was eighty-three years old at the time.

Afterwards, we were told that complications during the surgery had arisen, and that our mother had almost died on the operating table. Her blood pressure had dropped so dramatically, and had become so low, that adrenaline had had to be administered to save her life. We were also told that the cardiologist had encountered some problems during the operation whereby she was only able to successfully implant two of the three leads connected to the pacemaker, as a result of having experienced some unforeseen problems whilst trying to implant the third lead. And after making several failed attempts, she finally gave up after operating on our mother for a total of six hours in duration.

That night, we visited my mother in intensive care. Only two visitors were allowed at the one time. Never in my entire life had I ever seen my mother look so unwell before. Emotionally, seeing her in such a terrible state was extremely difficult for me to bear. My mother was in so much pain, in particular, every time she breathed. And she looked so weak and helpless lying there in the intensive care unit, barely able to talk. My nephew began to cry. He was so upset; he just couldn't bear to see his grandmother looking so unwell.

Penelope and I immediately regretted our decision in deciding to go ahead with the pacemaker implant for our mother. I was just so upset and terrified that our mother would not even make it through the night.

But she did make it through the night and the following day, my mother was transferred to a ward. I was relieved to see her looking so much better, but my mother was still in tremendous pain every time she breathed. Her chest area, where the pacemaker had been implanted, was still so painful. But it was most reassuring to see my mother in good spirits. However, her good progress was only short-lived.

Overnight, my mother experienced an episode of AF (Atrial Fibrillation) whereby her heart rate increased to be as high as 140 beats per minute. She was rushed to the Intensive Care Unit. My mother later told me that she now knows what it feels like to die.

She remained in Intensive Care for five days in total.

The day before my mother was actually due to be discharged from hospital, however, an ultrasound was performed to evaluate her heart function. But she experienced yet another setback, as a result of her operation.

After receiving a phone call at 11 pm that night from Penelope who was extremely distressed, anxious and upset, at the time, I too experienced similar emotions after she had informed me of our mother's most sudden deterioration in her heart health. Penelope told me that the doctor in charge of our mother's care in the Intensive Care Unit had called to inform her that the heart ultrasound had showed that there was now fluid surrounding her heart. Furthermore, he went on to explain that the fluid around her heart could either dissipate in a month's time or become worse, in which case the fluid would need to be removed with a syringe. Consequently, Penelope was beside herself with worry and grief, as was I.

We both regretted encouraging our mother to have the pacemaker implanted more than words can express. Penelope and I had both wished so desperately to improve our mother's quality of life; not make it worse. We never imagined that our mother would have experienced three consecutive complications as a result of her surgery, and I was shocked that we were not informed beforehand of any potential adverse effects that could arise from having this type of procedure. Our mother could have actually died as a result of her complications, and the mere thought of this frightened me to no end.

I was so upset and distressed that my mother had now developed fluid around her heart, especially at a time that she was scheduled to be discharged from hospital the following day. So, I prayed, with all of my heart and soul, to Our Lady and begged Her to help my mother. The Immaculate Virgin Mary had never let me down in the past, and She certainly failed to let me down during this particular time of crisis, as well.

In the morning, my mother underwent a repeat heart ultrasound. The fluid around her heart had miraculously dissipated! And as a result, my mother was discharged from hospital, as initially planned. I immediately knew that Our Lady had answered my prayers. Being a mother Herself, the Mother of God is so understanding, caring, empathetic and compassionate towards Her Children in Christ, and I was so incredibly grateful to Our Lady for having granted my petition.

Although the remainder of the year was rather uneventful, my father's health gradually deteriorated from Parkinson's disease, and towards the end of the year, he had even begun to experience some difficulties in swallowing. I visited my father weekly in the aged care facility. Sometimes, I brought him some home-cooked meals for lunch. He often struggled to feed himself, so I assisted him with his meals. My father really enjoyed eating home-cooked meals. He ate very slowly, and I could hear the sound of the food being swallowed with some difficulty. It was hard to watch my father struggling to swallow as he ate, and it saddened me tremendously. But despite his swallowing difficulties, my father still managed to eat most of his meals.

I became more and more depressed about my father's debilitating illness. It was difficult to watch him suffer, and deteriorate slowly from this insidious disease. After visiting my father, I would often become really depressed afterwards. I just couldn't help feeling this way. I felt so sorry for him, and I knew that he would only become even worse over time. But nevertheless, I continued to visit my father on a regular basis, and to become extremely melancholy afterwards.

To celebrate New Year's Eve, my sibling had organized for all of us to attend a New Year's Eve Ball which was being held in a function room near the top floor of a skyscraper in the city. A live band played some music whilst guests enjoyed a seafood buffet dinner. Overall, it was actually a really fun night. And at midnight, we watched the captivating and most beautiful display of fireworks that lit up the sky in the most brilliant colours. Some of the fireworks even appeared to resemble enormous exploding Christmas balls on a tree! And I will never forget my sibling's partner saying that the Year 2020 would be the best year ever! How wrong could he have been!

In January, my husband contracted a strange and most unusual virus exhibiting symptoms he had never experienced before. He felt feverish, was short of breath, had crushing chest pain, a red throat and burning eyes; Sam even struggled to breathe at night, and had to lie on his stomach in order to be able to breathe properly. He was also extremely lethargic for a considerable length of time, even after he had basically recovered from his illness.

There were even times when Sam considered calling an ambulance because he was feeling so unwell. Fortunately, Sam had a CPAP

(Continuous Positive Airway Pressure) machine for his sleep apnoea which helped him to breathe at night. Sam now believes that if he didn't require a CPAP machine for his medical condition, he would have had to go to hospital because Sam would not have been able to breathe on his own during the night.

After Sam recovered from his illness, he had an ECG and blood test to check on his heart function but all of the results came back as normal. In hindsight, we now firmly believe that my husband had actually contracted the coronavirus before it was known that this virus had already reached Australian shores.

About one week after my husband had initially contracted this virus, I felt extremely lethargic for about four consecutive days, so much so, that I literally had to psyche myself up into just getting out of my chair. Even walking my son to school required great effort on my part. I began to worry that there was something seriously wrong with me, and I had decided that if I didn't recover soon, I would have no choice but to seek medical assistance for my extreme lethargy. But I did fully recover within a period of about a week.

A short time afterwards, my son developed a runny nose, was lethargic and whenever he ran, Michael would develop a headache. He recuperated on the couch where he spent most of the day, lying down. So, I kept him home from school for about a week, as a result.

Soon afterwards, my daughter began to feel slightly unwell and even a bit nauseous, one morning, but she recovered very quickly and before long, life had returned to normal, for all of us, once more.

But then in March, we were informed by the media that the coronavirus had reached Australian shores. I was terrified of contracting this particular virus because the trigger for my episode of numbness a few years earlier was a stomach virus. I became afraid to leave the house. I avoided people at all costs. The number of coronavirus cases began to soar in my state. It was spreading like wildfire. We were averaging over 700 cases per day, the highest number in our entire country.

Our government decided that we needed to take drastic measures to combat this invisible enemy, and introduced a three-month lockdown period with a curfew being implemented for the evenings, as a result. It was an extremely strict lockdown, but I strongly believed at the time that there was no other option, and I truly welcomed this decision, as did many others in my state.

My children were busily engaged in remote learning at the time. Only my husband went out to go shopping, by himself. Many people panicked during this hard lockdown period, and engaged in the practice of panic buying. For some unknown reason, toilet paper was in very short supply during this period of time. In supermarkets, some people were even seen to be filling up their shopping trolleys to the brim solely with large amounts of toilet paper which would soon become a luxury item! As a result, my husband was forced to go from supermarket to supermarket in an attempt to secure even one packet of toilet paper for us when we had genuinely run out. And after he had finally managed to buy some at a particular store, one day, Sam came home looking most proud and victorious as he walked through the door, tightly hugging a packet of toilet paper against his chest!

Furthermore, the news, as reported on television, showed people in supermarkets actually stealing toilet paper right out of other people's shopping trolleys resulting in real physical fights erupting, as a consequence. We were currently living in the most bizarre times that I had ever experienced before, and I genuinely felt as though our entire world had literally been turned upside down, as if in an instant. I had absolutely no idea as to when our world would be able to return to its normal state, and when we could resume living our everyday lives in the way that we had become so accustomed to doing before the onset and worldwide spread of this deadly coronavirus pandemic.

# CHAPTER 13

Each morning, I awoke feeling most depressed and disheartened. I was, more often than not, consumed by negative thoughts directly related to the coronavirus pandemic and its consequences worldwide. I wondered if life, as we knew it, would ever be the same again.

And during this time, I had become quite heavily involved in using social media. I would upload posts regularly regarding my children's books, and try my utmost to entice people to purchase them. But my posts never seemed to really have much of an impact on the sales figures for my business. Many of the other users would often leave such positive feedback regarding my books, but to no avail since I would rarely make any sales from using social media.

One day, a businessman commented on one of my posts. It was a lovely comment which I really appreciated. He continued to comment on my posts on a regular basis and before long, we began to chat privately. Initially, he gave me the most valuable advice on how to market my books, as well as my business, which I gratefully accepted and put into practice immediately.

But then, we started talking about religion. He was Catholic, like myself, and he told me that he had actually read over 850 books about Saints. He seemed very knowledgeable in this area, and would often tell me the most interesting stories relating to the various Saints.

And when he enlightened me about a significant number of apparitions that had occurred in the early 1960's at Our Lady of Garabandal, I became rather shocked because I had never heard of these apparitions before.

He then advised me to conduct my own research on this topic, which I did, most obediently. Consequently, I discovered that Our Lady had appeared, in a number of apparitions, to four young girls in a little town located in Spain called Garabandal, many years ago and before I was even born.

The businessman then went on to state that as a consequence of these apparitions, a Miracle will take place during our lifetime. This miracle will comprise of a large cross which will be visible in the sky over Garabandal in the future on a specific date which has already been chosen by God. And this particular date will be announced eight days before the occurrence of this miracle by one of the four girls who witnessed the Garabandal Apparitions. Furthermore, light will emanate from specific locations on this large Cross in the sky depicting the five wounds that Jesus Christ suffered as a consequence of being nailed to the Cross during His Crucifixion.

In addition, he told me that before this miracle has occurred, every person in this entire world will experience a fifteen-minute interview with Jesus whereby all of the sins that we have committed in the past will be revealed to us, and we will feel great sorrow and remorse simultaneously for having committed these sins. We will also be told if we would have gone to Heaven or Hell if we had died on this particular day. And the purpose of all of these events, which will occur at a time which is not far off in the future, is to encourage all of us, as mortals on this earth, to repent and come back to God.

Furthermore, he said that after the interview has taken place, we will be given a certain amount of time to convert. But after this period has lapsed, Three Days of Darkness will dawn upon us during which time the sun will turn black, nothing will work during this period of time including electricity, and the Gates of Hell shall be opened for all of those mortals who have refused to repent despite having received multiple chances to convert.

In addition, all of the windows and doors in our homes will need to be covered so that we cannot look or see outside at all; otherwise, we shall perish. And since there will be no light, only candles made from beeswax will work during the Three Days of Darkness, and these candles must also be blessed by a priest beforehand.

It has also been highly recommended that we pray the Rosary in our homes, as much as possible, during this period of extreme darkness. As mentioned earlier, throughout the Three Days of Darkness, the Gates of Hell will be opened, and all of those who fail to convert will be taken directly to Hell.

And lastly, the businessman also informed me at the time that the Era of Peace will follow immediately after the Three Days of Darkness.

Then, one day, this businessman, named Gerry, actually told me that he was my Spiritual Director (SD). At this stage, I didn't even know what a Spiritual Director was since I had never heard of this term used before. But when I conducted my own research into this topic, I realized that Saints had Spiritual Directors. Gerry had hinted that God was calling me to become a Saint. So, I asked him directly if this was the case, and he promptly answered, "Yes!"

He had also informed me that I was on a journey in my Mystical Life and that only a few people in this world are blessed enough to be able to achieve this. He said that God had chosen me specifically because I love God above all things, and that this is what sets me apart from other religious Catholics worldwide.

Gerry then proceeded to ask me whether or not I intended to accept God's Call to become a Saint due to freewill and after procrastinating for only an extremely brief moment in time, I told him that I indeed did accept God's Call to become a Saint and I felt so incredibly happy, blessed, privileged and most honoured to have been chosen by God to become a Disciple of Jesus, serve Him and accept His Will.

I was totally shocked, however, by the things that Gerry was telling me at the time and I had initially found them most difficult to believe since I knew, deep down in my heart and soul, that I had not acquired any of the amazing qualities that Saints generally possess during their time on Earth. Although I was bestowed with the gift of faith by God, I viewed myself as being merely a sinner who was most unworthy of carrying such a prestigious title.

Eventually, Gerry admitted to me that he was a prophet. I was initially very wary of some of the things that he was telling me about the Catholic Faith but he never really seemed to say anything that was contrary to the teachings of the Roman Catholic Church, and so I had no real reason to disbelieve the new knowledge that he was imparting to me.

I told my husband all about this particular businessman that I had met through social media. I also informed Sam about the nature of my basic discussions with Gerry. Although Sam had advised me to be careful, and not to talk about our private life with him because he was, after all, a total stranger whom I had never actually met in person, my husband did not encourage me to disassociate from him in any way at this stage in my spiritual journey.

Gerry informed me that the coronavirus was a wake-up call from God, and that He was calling His People back to Him. Gerry discussed topics within Catholicism with so much conviction and authority that I believed him. He told me that I had to let go of my past, and the resentment that I harboured towards my father. And after careful consideration, I realized that he was absolutely right in his analysis of my current life situation.

As a result, I completely turned my life around from that moment onwards. I stopped swearing, and I began to pray on a daily basis - engaging in infused contemplation as opposed to praying out loud which is often how I used to pray in the past. Basically, I tried my utmost not to offend God in any way, and to become the best person that I could possibly be under the circumstances.

Over the next few months, I became extremely religious, even more pious than I had ever been before, and I was actually happy too – happier than I had ever been in the past, in fact. And during this period of time, I experienced a number of visions from God which are discussed in more detail, later in this book.

But in the meantime, my father had become extremely depressed as a result of the coronavirus pandemic since visiting restrictions were now being imposed in relation to aged care facilities. My father was extremely lonely without receiving his usual family visits that he had become so accustomed to experiencing on a regular basis. But there really was very little that we could do to appease his great loneliness due to the onset of this most frightening and new coronavirus pandemic.

Since the coronavirus infection rate in our state was peaking at over seven hundred per day, our government decided to enforce an extremely strict lockdown that we all had to observe, as mentioned earlier. And during this period of extreme lockdown, a staff member, from the aged care facility where my father was a resident, sent a photo of him to Penelope who became absolutely horrified the moment she had viewed the photo. My sibling immediately emailed the photo to me, and I was shocked to discover that our father had lost so much weight in such a relatively short period of time. He was so very thin and frail in the photo, and he appeared to look extremely unwell simultaneously. It was a stark contrast to the way I had remembered him the last time I visited my father at the aged care facility before the lockdown.

Penelope managed to organize, with the staff, permission to visit our father at the aged care facility but certain conditions were imposed on us, as a result, which accompanied this special privilege. They wheeled our father out into the back garden of the aged care facility in a wheelchair. We were only granted permission to gather together outside on the street, behind the back fence of the facility. I was shocked, most distraught and heartbroken to see our father looking so poorly; he was withering away before our very eyes, like a plant that was in desperate need of being watered. Our father virtually appeared to be at death's door.

And at this point in time, I found myself having to take a break from writing this book because emotionally, the memories of my father were just too painful for me to remember - memories which I had managed to somehow push to the back of my mind but which had now resurfaced, forcing me to have to relive them all over again. I began to question whether or not I was making the right decision in writing this book but after speaking to an old friend, I realized that I just had to continue writing my autobiography, not only for my own benefit but for the benefit of others who may find themselves on a similar life journey to mine.

My sibling, who had self-appointed herself to be in charge of all of our medical health, received a most distressing phone call regarding our father, one day. Penelope was informed that he had fallen over in the bathroom of all places and that our father had hurt himself. He had also sustained a head injury as a result of the fall.

My sibling immediately rushed over to visit him. He was wearing a bandage on his head to stop the bleeding, and we had no idea if he had sustained any other injuries, as well. An ambulance was called and he was taken to hospital for further investigation. For some unknown reason, staff only x-rayed his right hip which had not been damaged from the fall. He also underwent a brain scan which showed that he had actually experienced a small stroke in the past. My father was discharged after a relatively short hospital stay, and he was taken back to his room to recuperate at the aged care facility.

When I visited my father, after his fall, he appeared to be in a lot of pain. Since he barely had a voice now as a result of his advanced Parkinson's disease, I found it extremely difficult to communicate with him. Consequently, I felt quite frustrated and most distressed by this. I had specifically noticed that my father had become considerably worse after his fall and most alarmingly, his deterioration appeared to be quite rapid. And what made matters even worse during this time was that we were not allowed to visit my father whenever it suited us, due to the imposed coronavirus pandemic restrictions.

But then, not long after our father's fall, I received a most disturbing phone call from Penelope which will be etched in my memory forever. Our father's usual care doctor rang my sibling on this particular Sunday, during the month of August, to inform her that our father was dying. He asked Penelope if he should begin administering morphine to make our father more comfortable. My sibling rushed over to visit him, and emailed me a photo of our father. He looked absolutely horrendous, and as though he was a living corpse. Our father was so incredibly thin; he was literally just skin and bones, and really did appear to be dying. I struggled emotionally to see my father at this end stage of his life. My immediate thought was that we were not even told beforehand, by staff at the aged care facility, in relation to our father's most rapid deterioration until it had appeared to be almost too late.

And as a direct consequence of our father's alarmingly rapid deterioration in health, Penelope immediately arranged for our father's geriatrician to admit him into a private hospital, as a final attempt to save his life.

# CHAPTER 14

In the private hospital, staff inserted a drip into my father's arm since he was severely dehydrated, but still he was unable to really eat anything at all. I called him daily, and I was most grateful for the opportunity to be able to speak with my father on most occasions.

But on one such occasion, my father told me over the phone that he was nearly done, after I had asked him why he was not eating and drinking. I interpreted my father's most disturbing statement as he had already resigned himself to the fact that he was dying. And although this made me feel really sad, I still managed to retain a small ray of hope that my father would be able to recover from this terrible tragedy and get better over time.

And not long after my father had stated this, he said something to me on another occasion that I will never forget for as long as I live which actually broke my heart at the time. On this particular day that I had called my father, as I had become most accustomed to doing every day, he was actually too weak to be able to hold the receiver to his ear by himself. And therefore, a nurse assisted him in doing so, thus enabling me to be able to talk to him. I explained to my father how much we all loved him, and that we wanted him to get better as quickly as possible. He listened most intently and then after a while, my father said something to me in response that I just couldn't seem to understand at the time. And even just recalling this event now has caused me to become extremely emotional, so much so, that it has brought tears to my eyes.

At the end of the conversation, I asked the nurse if she knew what my father had said to me earlier. She replied that my father had told me that he loved me. And just hearing these words, immediately broke my heart and these were the last words that I would ever hear my father say to me.

And after reflecting on this, I firmly believe that my father knew that he was dying at the time. Eventually, the geriatrician told my sibling that although he had tried his utmost to save our father's life, since he was not responding to treatment and he was still unable to eat and drink anything at all, he had no other choice but to admit our father into a hospice where staff could make him more comfortable.

So, my father was placed in hospice care and after about three days, he passed away. On his death certificate, it stated that my father had died from pneumonia, dehydration, malnourishment, oesophagitis and Parkinson's disease.

We were all devastated. These conditions are treatable and perhaps my father could have lived longer if only we had known earlier. He had also sustained two fractures in his left pelvis as a result of his fall. Since the fall, it was apparent that my father was in rather intense pain afterwards, but I had no idea that his pain had stemmed from two fractures in his left pelvis, nor did anyone else, for that matter, since his left hip had not been x-rayed during his hospital stay directly after his fall.

My father's funeral was held almost two weeks after his death since my sibling was too distraught to be able to organize it any sooner. I nominated myself to be in charge of arranging the Church Service whilst my sibling organized the rest of the funeral arrangements.

Only ten people in total were allowed to attend his funeral due to the coronavirus restrictions that were in place during our severe lockdown period. None of Sam's family nor any of his relatives were able to attend my father's funeral, as a result.

I viewed my father in his coffin at the Church before the commencement of the funeral service. My father was almost unrecognizable. He was so thin, and his body literally looked as though it was just an empty shell. As I stared at my father, I was more than aware that his soul had already been separated from his body, and that he gone over to the other side. I had sincerely hoped that his soul was already in purgatory and that it would, sooner rather than later, progress to Heaven, being its final destination, which is where my family and I desperately aspire to go after we become deceased.

My only consolation in my father's passing, at this point in time, was that he was now at peace and his physical pain and suffering on Earth had finally come to an end.

I prayed to Our Lady and St Joseph (Her Spouse) for their intercession for my father's soul to be able to progress to Heaven as soon as possible, and to spare his soul from the Fires of Hell since the mere thought of his soul going to Hell was more devastating than I could possibly ever describe in words.

I had read a religious book once which described Hell in some detail, and just reading about it sent shivers up my spine, and made me absolutely terrified. What I had previously failed to recognize earlier is that souls who are sentenced to go to Hell, remain there for all eternity. They are never given the opportunity to progress to Heaven in the way that souls who go to purgatory first are destined to go eventually. The unbearable suffering and torture that souls undergo in Hell is relentless, permanent and infinite.

In stark contrast, however, the suffering that we may undergo as mortals on Earth is never permanent since our suffering, as we know it, comes to an abrupt end as soon as we become deceased.

And after reading this particular spiritual book, I decided that I possessed an immensely strong desire to aspire to go to Heaven after death, as my final destination. By going to Heaven, I would be able to be with God, and all of His Holy Angels and Saints, for all eternity.

The day after my father's funeral, I was walking on our treadmill at home whilst saying, "The Lord's Prayer", with my eyes closed, when suddenly, I felt an overwhelming love for Our Lord Jesus Christ. And then, most unexpectedly, I saw an extremely bright yellow Light which was almost too bright to look at even with my eyes closed. I immediately knew that this bright yellow Light had originated from Jesus, who is the Light of our World.

But as soon as this Light had disappeared, I experienced a crystal clear vision of Jesus on the Cross amidst a light green background; I could see only Jesus, who was nailed to an extremely large, life-sized brown Wooden Cross, in my line of vision. I noticed that His Head was tilted downwards, as if He had already died on the Cross. And since Jesus was life-sized in my vision, I immediately knew that Our Lord Jesus Christ, the only Begotten Son of our Lord and God, had appeared to me in the Flesh. And as I just stared at Him, on the Cross, the love that I experienced for Jesus was so extraordinarily intense and unbearably strong that I truly felt as though I wanted to die instantaneously just to be with Him. I didn't care about anything else in my life at that moment, only Jesus and I just wanted to be with Him for all eternity.

But as soon as this thought had crossed my mind, I realized that I was now struggling to breathe (and it's of the utmost importance here to note that I experienced absolutely no chest pain or pain of any sort during the entire duration of this vision). Surprisingly, however, I had initially still felt strangely at peace even though I was now struggling to breathe. But after a short while, I started to feel slightly afraid since I was now unable to breathe at all, and I truly felt as though I was dying. And it was at this exact point in time that the vision suddenly disappeared, and my breathing instantaneously returned to normal again.

I found it such an honour and privilege that Jesus had actually allowed me to experience His unconditional love, first-hand, through my vision, at which my soul had responded most involuntarily resulting in my genuine desire to wish to die at that moment to be with Jesus indefinitely. This vision was, without a doubt, one of the most powerful visions that I have ever experienced before which I will always cherish and treasure for a lifetime. The immense, extraordinary and intense love that I felt for Jesus during my vision will undoubtedly be firmly etched in my memory forever.

After experiencing this vision, I felt closer to Jesus, more than ever before. For years, I had always had a strong desire to be close to Jesus, but it was actually fear that had held me back. Since I knew that Jesus endured so much suffering during His Passion and Crucifixion, I was terrified of the consequences associated with becoming a Disciple of Jesus, namely the suffering involved, and to take up my own Cross and follow Him.

But looking back, I had actually endured so much prolonged emotional pain and torture during my life anyway, as well as extreme physical suffering at times, even though I had chosen not to follow Jesus for the reasons stated above. And I now feel so foolish for having suffered from such unjustified and irrational fears regarding becoming a Disciple of Jesus in the past. And in my heart, I truly believe that my suffering would have become so much more bearable and tolerable, if only I had chosen to follow Jesus much earlier in my life.

I firmly believe, without a doubt, that if more people in this world would make a conscious effort to really get to know Jesus at a spiritual level, and if they were to experience the intense love that He shares with each and every one of us, as I have been so blessed to be able to experience, they would find it impossible to reject Jesus, and not to love Him in return.

Being so spiritually close to Jesus as I am today, and through my own personal religious experiences, I have come to know Jesus as being most gentle, loving, loyal, consoling as well as infinitely patient at all times. He is always there for me whenever I need Him, especially during my times of trial and suffering and, over time, I have really grown to love Jesus above all things in my life. His Passion and Crucifixion are indicative of His infinite and unconditional love which Jesus shares with each one of us, and by

His Ascension, He reopened the Gateway to Heaven so that we may gain eternal life through Jesus Christ, our Lord and God.

During my times of trial and great suffering, I have also always prayed to God and/or Our Lady to assist me to overcome all of my difficulties. And yet, there is not a single time, during my lifetime, that God and Our Lady have not come to my aid. I have recently realized that although I have endured many illnesses and extremely difficult circumstances in my life, whereby I genuinely felt that I was pushed beyond my boundaries in terms of both physical and emotional suffering, I have successfully managed to overcome each and every one of these obstacles with the unfailing help of our Lord and God.

I know that God loves each one of us, even before we are conceived. Our Lord and God always gives us freewill, and by utilizing this freewill we can choose to either become a good or bad person and consequently, make good or poor choices in life.

Similarly, we can choose, by exercising this freewill, to become religious, follow Jesus and allow God to become a central part of our daily lives. Alternatively, we can choose not to be religious, become an atheist, or reject God completely and not include Him in our everyday lives.

Since I was about fifteen years of age, I had made the choice to include God in my daily life. Whenever bad things would happen, most regretfully, I would, more often than not, blame God for my mishaps. But when good things would happen in my life, I tended to thank God for showering me with His blessings.

I have always had faith in God of varying degrees, a holy fear of God and an extremely strong belief in God, as well as in supernatural occurrences. And I have been experiencing supernatural events in my life since my early twenties.

# CHAPTER 15

At the arrival of Father's Day, I was very sad due to my own father's passing less than a month earlier. But that night, I had a religious dream. And in my dream, I saw the face of a man who looked exactly like my father. The man was driving a white car (which I immediately recognized as being the same car that belonged to my father whilst he was still living independently at home) in what appeared to be a shopping centre carpark. He immediately found a parking space nearby, got out of his car and headed towards me. And it was at this exact moment that I identified this man as being my father, without a doubt. However, it's interesting to note here that although his hairstyle looked slightly different to the way it appeared before he died, his face was absolutely identical. He looked so healthy, displaying no signs of having Parkinson's disease or any other illness, for that matter. My father looked absolutely amazing, and his facial expression was one of true purpose in life.

As he walked briskly towards me, for he seemed to be in quite a hurry, I yelled, "Dad! Dad!" But my heart sank when my father appeared not to notice me at all, nor did he respond to my voice in any way. As he approached, I quickly reached out to grab my father's arm in an attempt to stop him from walking past me. But much to my dismay, my hands went straight through his body.

And it was only then that I realized that I had seen my father's soul. And after suddenly awakening from my dream, soon after, I became quite emotional since I missed my father terribly. By now, I was wide awake and after struggling to fall asleep again, I finally managed to do so, at last, but only after a considerable amount of time had passed.

The following day, I knew, without a doubt, that my dream was a message from God to reassure me that no longer did I have to worry about my father, since he had reached the other side and had gone to Heaven. It was such a comforting thought just to know that my father was now in God's care, and that he would be able to experience God's love in Heaven for all eternity.

Since the occurrence of this spiritual dream, I have been able to interpret the meaning in more detail. Firstly, the initial sight of my father driving his car is a representation of his soul being in a state of travel, and having left Purgatory.

Secondly, the circumstance of my father finding an immediate parking space, and then getting out of his car afterwards is a reflection of his soul having completed its journey in reaching its final destination, being Heaven.

And thirdly, my failed attempt at being able to grab my father's arm in passing, signifies that I saw my father's soul in my dream which had gone to Heaven on Father's Day.

Over the next few weeks, I experienced even more visions and spiritual experiences which I would like to discuss now in more detail.

One night, whilst fast asleep, I suddenly experienced a crystal clear vision of an olden-style musical instrument, but I am still baffled by its meaning and significance, even to this day. The musical instrument, which was made of pure gold, was shaped like an hourglass. There were also a number of horizontal golden strings attached across its entire body.

The following day, I conducted some online research on this musical instrument. Although I was unable to find the exact image that I had seen in my vision, I did manage to find some similar looking musical instruments named French Golden Lyre Harps.

Another most unusual supernatural experience happened over a year ago and occurred at around 9.30 pm in my loungeroom. On this particular night, whilst sitting on the couch next to my son, who was busy chatting with his sister and I at the time, I distinctly heard my first name being called out loud. But what I had found most peculiar was the fact that I had heard my name being called during my son's conversation with me. I couldn't understand why Michael had addressed me by my first name since it was so unlike him, and it had taken me by complete surprise.

After mulling this over, for a while, curiosity got the better of me and I asked my son why he had addressed me as Linda. Michael immediately replied that he had not called me by my first name, nor had he heard my name being called out loud, for that matter. And my daughter stated that she had not heard my name being mentioned in the conversation either.

I continued to question my son regarding this matter, several times, in fact, because I knew, without a doubt, that I had definitely heard my name being called out loud. But Michael continued to deny my allegations and since I knew that he never actually lied, I was left with no other choice but to believe him.

Shortly afterwards, I arrived at the strong realization that the humanlike voice that I had heard calling my name actually belonged to St Michael the Archangel who had communicated with me by means of locution. St Michael the Archangel had said my name in such a way as to gain my attention, but I had initially failed to look in the direction of where the voice was coming from until a short time later.

This was, in fact, the second time in my life that I had heard the voice of St Michael the Archangel. I wondered why he had called me by name but, in my heart and soul, I knew that St Michael the Archangel must have had a purpose in mind and I sincerely hoped that, one day, I would be able to find out in order to solve this great mystery.

I encountered another extremely special spiritual experience whilst I was kneeling and praying in front of my beautiful statue of Our Lady and Baby Jesus. I suddenly and most unexpectedly received a consolation from God in the form of a Holy Spirit Touch - a unique spiritual experience that I have always found most difficult to describe in words. It stirred intense emotion in my soul, and the feeling of love from Jesus almost brought me to tears. I struggled to recover from this Holy Spirit Touch for a considerable amount of time afterwards.

My supernatural experience is testament to the fact that Jesus loves each and every one of us so infinitely and unconditionally that it's far beyond the understanding of the human heart, and leaves our soul in desperate need of reciprocating God's love.

To my utter astonishment and surprise, however, I encountered a number of spiritual experiences involving St Michael the Archangel which I had not anticipated would ever happen to me because I know that in the entire history of the Roman Catholic Church, such occurrences are a rarity. And I truly feel more privileged and honoured for having experienced these spiritual encounters, than words can ever possibly hope to express.

And on this particular night, I experienced a sequence of visions regarding St Michael the Archangel. Upon experiencing my first vision of St Michael the Archangel (who is the Prince of the Nine Choirs of Angels and the Leader of God's Army of Heavenly Hosts which consists of billions of Angels whom God created even before the creation of Earth), I saw his wings, and I was impressed beyond words with their true magnificence, appearance and structure.

St Michael the Archangel most elegantly carries two pairs of exceedingly large and pure white feathery wings; one pair of his wings ascends upwards towards Heaven, whilst the other pair descends downwards towards Hell.

Shortly after experiencing my first vision of St Michael the Archangel, I was endowed with another vision containing more of an insight into the true physical appearance of this magnificent Archangel which is contrary to the images that I have seen online, and in any other material that may mention his name.

St Michael the Archangel carries a sword with a handle encased in gold. The sword, which is of immense height in length, has an extremely sharp curved tip which I imagine would be similar to the swords used in the Middle Ages to behead people, in particular, the early Christians.

A short time afterwards, I was made privy to another vision of St Michael the Archangel which encompassed the golden armour that he wears which I shall discuss in more detail shortly.

In each of my visions, God had granted me more and more of an insight into the true physical appearance of St Michael the Archangel. And at the completion of this remarkable set of visions, I was able to establish a most accurate image not only of the immense stature of St Michael the Archangel but also of his precise physical features.

St Michael the Archangel has shoulder-length, light brown wavy hair and large blue eyes. He wears a golden cuff around each of his extremely muscly arms with an engraved inscription which reads: 'Prince St Michael', and gold tunic armour. His enormous chest is encased in golden armour which is rippled specifically around his chest area, reflecting his pectoral muscles. St Michael the Archangel also wears short brown Roman sandals on his feet.

Furthermore, I experienced yet another vision of St Michael the Archangel which took me by complete surprise, whilst I was watching television with my family, one night. In all of his magnificence, St Michael the Archangel appeared in my vision to be in the process of landing, directly behind Our Lady, and I was in absolute awe of the enormous wing span of his outstretched wings. Our Lady was wearing a similar garment to that in my dream - Her veil was pale blue in colour, once again. But this time, the Mother of God looked young in appearance rather than old as in my dream.

But it is of the utmost importance here to strongly emphasize that at this particular point in time, I had, by now, become extremely pious - more spiritually happy than I had ever been in my entire life before.

And although I am blessed for having experienced so many visions, spiritual dreams and supernatural occurrences, I have also encountered the most horrifying and terrifying experiences of my life as a result of brief visitations from Satan Himself - two of which I would now like to take this opportunity to briefly discuss in this book.

I shall never forget, for as long as I live until the day I die, the time that I was fast asleep, one night, and I suddenly awoke from a sensation that someone had actually grabbed my left ankle and was beginning to drag me off my bed and onto the floor. I was absolutely terror-stricken, and I froze in fright. I was unable to move. It was as though my body was paralysed with fear and I didn't know what to do or how to save myself since I knew that Satan Himself had actually grabbed my leg and wished to physically drag me out of bed and terminate me. But after a few short seconds had passed, Prince St Michael actually came to my rescue like a 'Knight in Shining Armour', and Satan immediately let go of me, and left the room.

And after this paralytic encounter with Satan Himself, I had another brief supernatural occurrence with him. But on this occasion, I was merely sitting at my computer working on my autobiography when I suddenly felt terror-stricken, once more, and I immediately knew that Satan Himself had most unexpectedly appeared before me. I had a severe panic attack and I called upon my Lord and God's Name, Jesus Christ, in desperation, and He unfailingly helped, protected and saved me from Satan who then immediately left my presence, as a result.

A tell-tale sign that Satan has most unexpectedly appeared in your presence is when you suddenly experience feelings of immeasurable panic, you're terror-stricken and paralysed with fear; your body then starts to shake uncontrollably out of fright and although your first instinct is to run, common sense prevails by telling you that you can't hide or escape from Satan on your own accord without God's help, and you can actually feel each hair on your arms and legs, in particular, standing upright from being absolutely petrified of being trapped, hurt and/or terminated by Satan Himself.

# CHAPTER 16

It's important to emphasize here that God gives us the freewill to do as we please in life – we can choose to either include and follow Jesus or exclude Him from our daily lives.

As a result of my strong conversion, I turned to God to the extreme, and I became more religious than I had ever been in my entire life before.

In the past, whenever I became ill, was desperately unhappy about something in particular, or even if a family member had become ill, my first instinct was to pray to God and/or Our Lady for their help. And my prayers were always answered. They never let me down, not even once, and we always recovered from our illnesses/afflictions, as a result.

My behaviour changed quite dramatically at the time of my conversion. As a direct consequence of being unable to make my own decisions in life due to pressure from extended family members, I felt a strong need to turn to God to the extreme in order to be able to experience true happiness.

I stayed up all night praying to God. I saw supernatural signs, consisting of a Rosary in particular, which was swaying back and forth in the dark on my religious statue of Our Lady holding Baby

Jesus, and I experienced other supernatural events and visions that no one else in my family was able to see, only me.

But shortly after the occurrence of these supernatural events, I encountered yet another spiritual experience which took me by complete surprise.

One morning, whilst in our rumpus room upstairs, I saw a message written on the wall – it was a personalized message that had been written especially for me. The message covered a considerable portion of the wall; it was written in large fancy handwriting, and the message was decorated so elaborately. I immediately knew that this message had been written by an Angel of God – St Michael the Archangel, in fact, whom I was extremely spiritually close to at the time, and whom I love very much. Although the message was written in white, it was still extremely visible, crystal clear, in fact, against the cream-coloured wall. And the message read: "Congratulations Linda on becoming a Saint."

I became extremely excited after reading this amazing and most unexpected message. My immediate thought at the time was to call my two children into the rumpus room so that they too would be able to read and admire this most special message.

But I was utterly astonished when Therese and Michael were both unable to view the message. Instead, they just stared at a blank wall. The message was not actually visible to them, only to me. I questioned my children at length, over and over again, because I just couldn't understand why they were unable to view this message that I could see so clearly. As a result, I finally made the assumption that perhaps they were not religious enough to be able to view this message like I could.

I then proceeded to call my husband to read the message since I believed that surely he would be able to see this personalized message that had been written by St Michael the Archangel, especially for me. But Sam also failed to be able to view the message. Instead, he merely stared at a blank wall, just like both of my children had done earlier. I simply couldn't understand why I was the only person in my family who was able to see and read this most beautiful message, and to say that I was stunned by this revelation would be a gross understatement.

During this time, my husband and children stared at me as though I was crazy, and I strongly believe that they actually did, in fact, think that I was crazy at the time. However, soon afterwards, I realized that the message that was written by St Michael the Archangel was, in fact, a vision which was solely meant to be experienced by me personally, and no one else in my family.

However, on this same day, to my absolute shock, utter horror and dismay, I was admitted, against my will, to a mental health ward in a public hospital for nine consecutive days from which I was finally released and allowed to go home on the tenth day.

Whilst in the process of being admitted to hospital, I underwent a brain scan, the results for which showed that my scan was unsurprisingly, totally normal in appearance.

But during my entire hospital stay, I was absolutely terrified, particularly at the very beginning. I was, more often than not, too afraid to venture out into the corridor or to visit the common room where the majority of the other patients gathered, and ate their daily meals. Mostly, I ate my meals by myself in my own room, whenever possible.

I had observed that it was common practice for most of the other patients to either talk or sing songs out loud to themselves whilst walking up and down the corridors in my ward. I knew, without a doubt, that I did not belong in this hospital, but I had no way of escaping from this most frightening and horrific place which I likened to being a prisoner trapped in jail. I was totally unlike the other patients, both in my behaviour and intellect. I remained isolated in my room, as much as possible, since I constantly feared for my own safety, despite the fact that the other patients didn't appear to engage in aggressive behaviour.

I had brought my son's Rosary with me to the hospital in order for Our Lady to protect me during my stay. In the daytime, I wore it around my neck but at night, I fell asleep with the Rosary tightly clenched in my hand. I prayed constantly to Our Lady, Jesus, St Michael the Archangel and to God.

Whilst in hospital, I missed my family more than words can possibly express, and I desperately wanted to be discharged, as soon as possible, so that I could go home and just be with them, once more.

I worried about my husband and children immensely, particularly in relation to my children and how they were coping at home without me. But I knew that Sam was a wonderful father, and that he would be taking the best possible care of them whilst I was away. In addition, I was sure that my husband would also provide them with much needed support at all times.

During my hospital stay, I had a lot of free time on my hands which forced me to re-evaluate my life, and to try to work out how on earth I had ended up being a patient in this horrendous place.

In the end, psychiatrists diagnosed me with first brief-reactive psychosis. But in my view, and in my heart and soul, I always knew that there was never anything actually wrong with me mentally at the time. Furthermore, I strongly believe that there is no way in this world that God would ever allow someone whom He has entrusted with so many of His visions, religious dreams and spiritual experiences to be psychotic in any way, shape or form.

Despite the fact that I viewed myself, at this point in time, as being solely a mother and wife, a nobody, an unimportant, insignificant and worthless human being in this world, I have been experiencing visions, religious dreams and spiritual experiences on an ongoing but intermittent basis for over fourteen years now. I have grown to love Jesus and God above all things in my life; I have always held a most holy fear of God; an extremely strong belief in God, and I have continually turned to Him for help during my time of need.

Admittedly, there were times in my life in which my faith had wavered considerably which induced feelings of intense unhappiness, great distress and desolation for me. But during other times, I had managed to possess an unshakeable faith in God for extended periods of time.

I have always had a strong belief in the supernatural, since early childhood, in fact, and in my own personal Guardian Angel whom I know is continuously looking after and protecting me, every day of my life.

I have always known that God Himself is both Divine and

supernatural in nature and I have continuously, and without a doubt, been extremely drawn to God for my entire life.

I have had to endure unbearable emotional suffering and torture, for more than half of my life; I have now made the personal choice to carry the Cross for Jesus, as a result of my own freewill. I have chosen to do God's Will and forfeited my own will simultaneously due to my intense love for Jesus, and in gratitude for the great blessings that God has bestowed upon me, namely my husband and children but also, as a result of my countless visions, religious dreams and spiritual experiences which will be etched in my memory and cherished forever.

To say that I was relieved when I was finally discharged from hospital would be a gross understatement. I was so incredulously happy to be home, and to be with my beloved family, once again, where I felt that I belonged, so much so, that there are no words in the English vocabulary that could adequately describe my feelings of immense joy at that moment in time.

I consulted with a therapist privately for a very short period of time after I was discharged from hospital.

During my second visit, I was assessed as no longer requiring my therapist's services anymore.

I was merely a product of my environment and consequently, I had become a failure in terms of my career since I lacked the self-confidence to be able to market and promote my own children's books effectively, and I continually viewed myself as being an unimportant, insignificant and worthless human being who was incapable of ever becoming successful at anything in life.

Almost immediately after arriving home from hospital, I was terrified to become spiritual again, for fear of being sent back to hospital, despite the fact that I had desperately felt the need, deep in my heart and soul, to be extremely pious again. And this lack of freedom was a form of real emotional torture for me at the time.

# CHAPTER 17

As mentioned earlier in this book, I have been religious since I was about six years old. I have always turned to God in my hour of need and whenever obstacles had, suddenly and most unexpectedly, been thrown in my path. And never once has God not helped me to overcome my challenges in life; and never once has God not answered my prayers.

God has always been there for me whenever I have needed Him the most, without fail. Sometimes, my prayers would be answered almost immediately, whilst at other times, my prayers would only be answered after an extended period of time had passed.

Similarly, in order for some of my petitions to be granted by God, I would only have to pray once. And yet for other petitions, I would need to pray multiple times in order for my particular prayers to be answered by God.

And I would like to emphasize here that I believe that my prayers to God, and Our Lady, have always been answered in the past, due to my extremely strong belief in God, faith in God and the fact that I have always known, in my heart and soul, that God can do absolutely anything and that nothing is impossible through God.

No matter how impossible something may seem to mankind

(since we are, after all, but mere mortals, temporarily living on this extraordinary earth that God, Who gave us life, so generously created for all of us to share and enjoy), nothing is impossible through our Lord Jesus Christ Who is the Light of our world, and the Way, the Truth and the Life.

'To know Jesus is to love Him' was the catalyst that I needed in order for me to consequently be able to enjoy and focus more fully on all of the many blessings that God had already bestowed upon me in my life, namely my husband and children, as well as my countless visions, religious dreams and spiritual experiences.

Since Our Lady's appearance to me in my personal Apparition, for years I had struggled to interpret the true meaning of my dream. And I often wondered about the important messages that Our Lady had relayed to me that night which I had failed to fully understand at the time, until after the prophecy had come true which was more than six years later.

For months after my recent hospital admission, I was unable to understand and comprehend why I had had to undergo such great suffering by being forced to go to hospital against my will. Practically every single day, I struggled to come to terms with this fact, and I honestly felt as though it had totally ruined my life forever; that I would never be able to put this experience behind me, no matter how hard I tried, and that this trial would haunt and upset me for the rest of my life until the day I died. I felt so ashamed and embarrassed about what had happened to me, and I kept this a secret from everyone that I knew. I just didn't have the courage to tell anyone about my forced hospital stay; I didn't really know how to deal with this or how I could successfully put it behind me so that I would be able to move forwards with my life or at least make an attempt to move forwards with my life, and leave my painful and torturous past behind me.

And then, one day, I suddenly had a revelation. For the first time, my dream about Our Lady was finally beginning to make sense to me, at last. My dream had, in fact, been a prophecy of an event which was going to take place in the future that involved me personally. I had actually sensed that something bad was going to happen from the expression on Our Lady's face when she had looked directly at me and stared into my soul with such intensity. But I had absolutely no idea as to what this might be.

Looking back, I am most thankful to God for preventing me from being able to work out the true meaning of my dream until after the horrendous event had actually occurred, and I was given the opportunity to be able to recover from my emotionally excruciating ordeal.

And at this point in time, in my life journey, I believe that the interpretation of my dream is as follows:

At the beginning of my dream, St Michael the Archangel made an announcement that Hail Mary was going to hospital. And whilst experiencing this dream, I had actually thought this to be most peculiar at the time since I knew that Our Lady would never become ill, and that She certainly would never have to seek hospital treatment of any kind.

By now, I had worked out the true meaning behind St Michael the Archangel's message: Upon being admitted to hospital, I brought my son's Rosary with me, praying constantly to Our Lady during my hospital stay. The Rosary represents Our Lady, and She encourages people to pray the Rosary to Her as often as possible. And, in doing so, it has even been said that those who pray the Rosary regularly will receive additional blessings in their lives from God.

Furthermore, it is also customary for St Michael the Archangel to always announce the arrival of Our Lady, and my dream was no exception.

The brown building in my dream was of a similar colour to the hospital building in which I had stayed as a patient. The counter that Our Lady stood behind, represented the hospital counter in my ward. The stairs in my dream were a representation of the stairs that I had to climb in order to reach my hospital ward from the ground floor.

I have realized that during the time at which Our Lady had stood diagonally opposite but failed to glance at me, and Penelope had called me away from the Blessed Virgin Mary to look up at the sky, this could be interpreted as my sibling's attempts at preventing me from becoming as religious as I had always felt the need to be, especially in relation to the period directly after returning home from hospital.

If I were to even briefly mention God and/or Our Lady in passing conversation or talk about religion in any way, for that matter, to my sibling, she would immediately think that I was having a 'relapse', and that I should be re-admitted to hospital. And so, this was the dilemma that I was now being confronted with on a daily basis, and this lack of spiritual freedom was slowly destroying my spirit, and was having a most detrimental effect on my soul. I started to become extremely frustrated and depressed. I truly felt as though I was being restrained, and that life had no meaning for me anymore.

I desperately, and more than anything else, needed to become close to Jesus again, since God had always been the centre of my life and I knew, without a doubt, that I simply could not live without Him.

My mother-in-law as well as my own mother had also told me that I was too religious after my conversion and they had all tried to take me away from God and to divert me from the path of righteousness which I had chosen to follow instead of going down the path which leads to destruction.

The fake clouds, in my dream, that Penelope was so mesmerized by represent her obsession with worldly matters, material possessions, position and status.

And when Our Lady finally turned to look at me, wearing a most concerned look on Her face, and appeared to stare straight into my soul, this signifies the prophecy of my being admitted to hospital, six years later, against my will. The Blessed Virgin Mary knew that I would suffer tremendously, not only during my forced hospital stay but for quite some time afterwards and consequently, this is also why Our Lady initially appeared to look old in my dream which represents great suffering in life.

However, by becoming young again towards the end of my dream, the Mother of God not only revealed Herself to me, but a crucial element that is most worthy of being noted here is that this also provided me with a reassurance that my extreme suffering in life will come to an end at some time in the future.

After the occurrence of my dream though, I no longer felt as close to Our Lady as I had in the past and this alone, caused me to experience much grief, sadness and unrest in my soul. The distance that I had placed between myself and the Immaculate Virgin Mary during this time was as a result of a nagging feeling that Our Lady had a really important message to relay to me which had not actually been communicated in my personal Apparition, however.

But after a period of six years had passed, this prophecy became reality when I was admitted to a mental health ward in a hospital, against my will. And this was, in fact, the most traumatic experience of my entire life, and I never thought that I would ever be able to put this horrendous and torturous experience behind me, for the remainder of my existence on this earth.

Interestingly enough though, I did become extremely close to Our Lady again, but only after a period of six years had lapsed, and it was at the beginning of the same year in which I would later be admitted to hospital. During my hospital stay, I prayed to Our Lady constantly, and She helped me to overcome my most traumatic trial, as did Jesus Christ, our Lord and God, and St Michael the Archangel.

But I will always regret, for the rest of my life, not having told Our Lady that I loved Her, in my dream, since I feel that Her appearance to me in a personal Apparition was a once in a lifetime opportunity that I may never be blessed enough to be able to experience ever again.

Upon arrival at home from hospital, I initially felt extremely happy and grateful to be reunited with my beautiful family again. But soon afterwards, I became disillusioned with my life and I genuinely felt as though my hospital stay had been a severe punishment from God, for an unknown sin which I believed that I must have committed in the past.

I began to distance myself from God, more and more. However, as a direct consequence of this, I inadvertently felt totally lost, angry, frustrated, disillusioned with life, resentful, extremely unhappy and so alone in my suffering. And during this period, I truly felt as though no one in this entire world would possibly be able to understand the trauma and tremendous amount of emotional torture that I was experiencing at the time, resulting from my forced hospital stay and for having disassociated myself from God Who had always been there for me in my time of need, and Who had always been the centre of my life. Without God playing a central role in my life, I now felt more afraid than ever before.

I was in such a bad frame of mind that I felt as though I was no longer able to be religious anymore, since I knew that God could have prevented my forced hospital admission, and that He had actually allowed this to happen to me, since it was obviously God's Will that I be admitted to hospital. I even began to question God's love for me at the time. I felt as though this incident had ruined my life completely and forever, and that I would never be able to experience true happiness in my life, ever again, as a result.

In desperation, I made an appointment with a Catholic priest for a chat because I didn't know who else I could turn to under these most difficult circumstances, and I truly felt as though my faith in God was not only dwindling but was now in dire straits. For all of my life, I had possessed such a strong belief in God and always turned to God in my hour of need. And it really scared me, more than words can possibly express, that I suddenly felt a real desire to turn away from God.

After our meeting, I was left feeling rather despondent, and as though our chat was not as productive as I had initially hoped. But although this particular priest had, in fact, helped me to a lesser degree, I still didn't feel comfortable telling him everything that was on my mind and in my heart at the time.

So, I ended up consulting with another priest whom I clicked with immediately. I felt so incredibly comfortable talking to him and after our meeting, I honestly felt as though he had really helped me to strengthen my faith. And this same priest was, in fact, responsible for bringing me back to God, once more.

The new Catholic priest became the Spiritual Director that I had so desperately needed in my life at the time. He played a most significant role in the saving of my faith, including my spiritual relationship with God, and I regret so much that I had questioned God's love for me, earlier on, simply because I had failed to understand the bigger picture and God's Mysteries.

Initially, I failed to understand why God had allowed such a traumatic event to happen to me, namely my forced hospital admission, since I had always considered myself to be such a religious person of Faith. And I certainly had never expected to have to live through such a traumatic experience in my life.

I began to meet with my new Spiritual Director on a regular basis. We discussed my trials, tribulations and great suffering in life, my visions, religious dreams and spiritual experiences. He explained my life events in detail, from his perspective, and through his own spiritual wisdom which always made perfect sense to me at the time. I looked forward to our sessions so very much, and I found that my new Spiritual Director was able to help me more than anyone else ever could. I was in absolute awe of his spiritual enthusiasm and love for Jesus which was infectious. In my eyes, he was the perfect priest and I believed, without a doubt, that he had found his true calling in life.

And this particular priest had also informed me that I was a Mystic. I had actually already perceived this to be true but it was most reassuring to get verification for my mysticism from a priest whom I respected so much and held in such high regard.

During one of our sessions, I finally mustered up the courage to tell my Spiritual Director about my forced hospital admission, a few months earlier. And I distinctly remember having also told him that I truly felt at the time that I would never be able to put this horrific experience behind me for as long as I lived. But he reassured me that, in time, I would, in fact, be able to put this whole incident behind me. And in the end, he was proved right.

Furthermore, when my Spiritual Director told me that he didn't believe that I was ever psychotic, I felt most reassured and much happier as a result. My Spiritual Director knew that, since I was a Mystic, I experienced supernatural events and had spiritual experiences that others could never possibly understand unless they were Mystics themselves.

Immediately after arriving home from hospital, I had struggled to comprehend how God could have allowed someone like me, who was experiencing constant but intermittent visions, religious dreams and spiritual experiences, to ever become psychotic.

And deep down, in my heart and soul, I always knew that I was never psychotic because I have been experiencing supernatural events in my life since my early twenties.

## CHAPTER 18

I began to meet with the priest on a weekly basis. I honestly felt as though I wouldn't feel as comfortable discussing really personal matters with any other priest, and that I could never trust anyone else in the same way that I had grown to trust my new Spiritual Director. I felt so drawn to him because in my view, he was such a Holy priest, and I quickly realized that God had brought him into my life for a purpose - to assist me to become spiritually closer to God which was definitely something that I had so desperately craved since my release from hospital. And deep down in my soul, I had always known this to be a need rather than a want in life.

And when my Spiritual Director (SD) told me, during one of our sessions, that he believed in me, I became rather emotional at the time, since it meant more to me than words can ever possibly express. No one else, in this entire world, had ever said this to me before, and just knowing that my SD believed in me, was the catalyst in causing me to actually start believing in myself.

I slowly regained my faith in God, and in Jesus. And the closer I became to Jesus, the happier I started to become. I began to love Jesus and God above all things, once again. I had suddenly arrived at the realization that I would never be able to experience true happiness without God playing a most significant and central role in my life since Jesus was truly the essence of my being. Jesus was definitely and indisputably, a part of me and my existence. I felt as though God really was living in my soul.

During my lifetime, I have experienced both sides of the spectrum in terms of life with, and without God as being a part of it. I had felt so desolate, empty and lost during the times that I had rejected God. As a consequence, I was overwhelmed and overshadowed by feelings of anxiety, unrest, fear, helplessness and more misery than I can express in words. I truly felt as though I was a lost sheep who desperately needed to find their shepherd in order to be able to feel secure, loved and protected, once more.

But during the times when I had felt really close to God, I experienced true happiness and peace in my soul. When bad things occurred in my life, I felt so reassured and comforted just to know that God always had the potential to help me, even when no one else could.

In my heart and soul, I had already arrived at the strong realization, by now, that God did, in fact, play a most crucial role in my life, and that Jesus was the key component in providing me with true happiness in life. Not only did God have the ability to alleviate my fears and anxieties in life, but He also provided me with the reassurance that I had always so desperately needed to receive, especially during my times of trial and suffering - that I was never actually alone since Jesus was always with me, and that He would constantly be there to comfort, support and help me whenever I needed Him.

And I regret so much that I had not arrived at this realization earlier in life, and that it had actually taken me 52 years to finally work this out for myself.

Even today, I am still experiencing such a tremendous feeling of guilt for having abandoned God at certain times in my life when He never once, abandoned me. I feel so foolish and remorseful for being so unenlightened about God in the past. And as a result, I have developed such a strong desire to become a faithful and loyal Disciple of Jesus, live my life in accordance with the Way, the Truth and the Life and carry out God's Will for the remainder of my life until I become deceased and pass from this life and into the next.

I have been most privileged to be able to experience God's love as a result of my life-sized vision of Jesus on the wooden Cross which occurred over a year ago now. There are no words in the English language that can adequately describe the intense love that Jesus shares with each and every one of us. His love is always unconditional and infinite. And if there was one word that I could use to describe God it would be 'Love' since God is Love.

God always provides us with His love, comfort, reassurance, hope, peace and infinite mercy. He is also responsible for the creation of many great miracles, and is always able to provide us with His assistance even when nobody else on this earth is able to help us.

Jesus never gives up on us, even during the times that we may have given up on Him. He always gives us multiple chances to repent and continues to love us unconditionally, even when we may fail to reciprocate His love and have excluded Jesus from our lives.

God does answer our prayers when we turn to Him for help, in spite of the fact that we may sometimes perceive that our prayers have remained unanswered.

And I would like to take this opportunity to strongly emphasize that God always sees the bigger picture which we are not usually privy to and as a consequence, we must learn to accept God's Will if our prayers have not been answered in the way that we had initially hoped, and arrive at the realization that this is a part of God's Mysteries.

It's also most noteworthy to take into consideration the fact that sometimes, it requires multiple prayers over an extended period of time for a particular prayer to be answered. And we should always try to retain hope in any given situation since God is Hope, and by holding onto our faith we are retaining hope.

I find it most reassuring to know that nothing can occur in this world unless it's either God's Ordained Will or His Permitting Will since God created our world, and every single object and/or living thing that exists in it.

It's God's intention to always try His utmost to save each and every one of our souls and in doing so, we shall be granted the greatest honour and privilege of being able to join God in Eternal Paradise which was reopened for us by His Only Begotten Son, Our Lord Jesus Christ, as a result of His Passion and Crucifixion. And as a consequence of His Passion, Crucifixion, Death and Resurrection, Jesus bequeathed to mankind the greatest gift that could ever have been bestowed upon us - the opportunity to be able to experience God's love in its purest form, peace, comfort and an everlasting happiness in Heaven for all eternity.

But I would like to emphasize at this point in time that it actually pleases God when we need Him, turn to Him for help, and include God in our everyday lives.

We should never be afraid to follow Jesus and become one of His Disciples, as I was for so many years, since the rewards that we shall receive from God in the Kingdom of Heaven, and as mortals on this earth, are immeasurable and are so great that our own human brains are most incapable of even being able to conceive, possibly imagine or ever understand.

The intense love that Jesus shares with each one of us is indescribable, unconditional and infinite. Since our souls were made to need love, and by drawing on my own personal life experiences, I have adopted the strong belief that what genuinely gives us true happiness in life is, in fact, 'love', and to be loved for the person that we actually are and were destined to become.

I feel that it's of the utmost importance here to emphasize that we must not live our lives solely to please our family members, friends or others that we may encounter in our everyday lives. But instead, we should always possess the fortitude to remain true to ourselves no matter how difficult this may be under our current life circumstances.

I have always so desperately needed to feel loved during my lifetime, especially since I never really felt truly cherished as a child growing up.

The love that Jesus shares with each and every one of us is of much greater intensity than the love that we, as mere mortals, can ever receive or experience from another human being on this earth.

In my vision in which I witnessed Jesus on the Cross, life-sized and in the Flesh, the love that I felt for Him, at the time, was so intense that I had truly wanted to die instantaneously just to be with Jesus forever.

But I also feel that it's of extreme importance here to emphasize that I have never felt this way during my entire life before. I have always had such a strong desire to live my life to the fullest. I have continually wanted to be the best mother and wife that I can possibly become as well as a good role model for my family, and to live to a ripe old age since I have always felt that people who are able to live to ninety years are so blessed, and have attained such a great achievement in life.

It would give me such great happiness to be responsible for assisting all of my family members to become as pious as possible, to follow my example spiritually, and for my entire family to love God above all things, as I do now, since I would be absolutely devastated if one or more of my family members failed to go to Heaven as their final destination. I love my husband and children so unbearably much; I love spending time with them more than words can ever possibly hope to express, and I would love to be given the opportunity to spend all of eternity with my family in Heaven.

Recently, the other night, I experienced another religious dream. And in this particular dream, I was standing on a wooden bridge which had water underneath it. In the distance, I saw a light green crocodile that was extremely oversized in appearance and nature. It was resting against the left riverbank which was encompassed by sedimentary rock formations. Shortly afterwards, the crocodile began to launch slightly away from the riverbank before opening its huge jaws, exposing all of its extremely sharp and pointy teeth. However, most interestingly though, I would like to strongly emphasize that I did not experience any fear in my dream at this point in time nor at any other point, for that matter.

Almost immediately afterwards, the crocodile closed its jaws, nestled back against the riverbank and proceeded to sink almost entirely beneath the water with only the top portion of its back remaining visible.

During the next stage of my dream, I suddenly felt someone's hand hold my right hand firstly, and then somebody held my left one so that both of my hands were, in fact, being held, tightly and firmly, simultaneously. At the time, it had truly felt as though human hands were holding mine, since I had felt, without a doubt, the physical sensation, as well as the pressure, associated with holding human hands. Again, I would like to emphasize that I felt no fear at this point in time either but rather, I experienced a feeling of only peace, comfort and reassurance instead.

However, as soon as the physical sensation associated with my hands being held had ceased to exist, I experienced a subsequent vision in my dream which encompassed a pair of humanlike hands, folded one on top of the other, and I immediately noticed that the hands were much larger in size than that of mortal human hands. And soon after this vision had disappeared, I suddenly awoke from my dream.

I knew, without a doubt, that someone had definitely held both of my hands in my dream. I would like to emphasize at this point that I did not feel afraid when I awoke, and I couldn't stop thinking about the tight grip that I had felt when my hands were being held so firmly in my dream.

I immediately knew that the extremely large pair of hands belonged to St Michael the Archangel. And I distinctly remember wondering whether this magnificent Archangel had actually held both of my hands in my dream. But I later realized that Jesus (Who has been holding my hand continuously throughout all of my trials and tribulations in life) had held my left hand, whilst St Michael the Archangel had held my right one.

And this reminds me of the time that I went for a walk with my mother in the rain, one afternoon, and found a religious icon of the Crucifix of Jesus lying in the gutter in the muddy water.

After initially having noticed the Cross of Jesus, walked past it and then backtracked in order to pick up this Crucifix, I had believed at the time, without a doubt, that Jesus did not deserve to be lying in the gutter. And so, feeling an overwhelming need and desire to save Him, I picked up the religious icon, and held the Crucifix of Jesus tightly in my hand, during my entire walk.

Upon returning home, however, I remember carefully and lovingly washing and cleaning the Crucifix of Jesus that I had found, and I treasured this most special religious icon more than words can express.

And as a direct result of having both found and picked up the Crucifix of Jesus lying in the gutter, it was made privy to me afterwards that it was actually Jesus Who had held my left hand in my dream since I had held the Crucifix tightly in my left hand during the walk in the rain, and the umbrella in my right hand.

Furthermore, I have worked out since the occurrence of my dream that the oversized crocodile in the water was a representation of the devil. The bridge that I was standing on signified my life journey. The hands that held my hands so firmly and tightly belonged to

Jesus and St Michael the Archangel. It's obvious to me that it had strongly felt as though human hands were holding my hands in my dream because both Jesus and St Michael the Archangel are real, and I bear witness and testimony to their existence through the numerous supernatural events that I have experienced in the past.

# CHAPTER 19

But a strong realization which I had failed to initially arrive at earlier is that Jesus has been, in fact, continually with me, holding my hand, especially during all of my trials and tribulations in life, and even during the times when I was unaware of His presence.

Recently, however, I have also come to realize that in the past, when I had distanced myself from Jesus, He was still always there for me when I had needed Him the most. I am so ashamed to admit that I had abandoned Jesus, and was too afraid to become spiritually close to Him as a result of my irrational fears relating to the great suffering that I believed would occur if I were to take up my Cross and follow Jesus. But despite my great failings, Jesus has never abandoned or given up on me during my lifetime.

I remember reading in a spiritual book recently that all mortals on this earth experience an element of suffering during their lifetime, regardless of whether they believe in God or not. But what I had previously failed to recognize until now is that if I had chosen to follow Jesus earlier in my life, and become more spiritually close to Him, He would have helped to ease my burden and alleviate my pain and suffering, so much more, which would have resulted in my circumstances becoming more tolerable and bearable at the time.

But does my life story really end here? Have I arrived at enough revelations and realizations to now be able to experience true happiness in life?

Well, I feel as though I have definitely become a happier person as a result of having arrived at the strong realization that Jesus is always with me, and is holding my hand throughout my life journey. But I still have an inkling that my life story doesn't actually end here, and that perhaps my happiness has not yet reached its full potential.

So, I have decided that I will not publish my book, as yet, at this point in time, just in case I receive more beneficial revelations and/or spiritual experiences which would not only enhance my life but would also reduce my great suffering to an even lesser extent.

Taking into account all of my life experiences to date, I have realized that the suffering that I have had to endure over the past 52 years was all worthwhile - just to have been granted the greatest honour and privilege by God of being able to experience the life-sized vision of Jesus on the Cross alone, over a year ago now. I feel most blessed, beyond words, that Jesus had actually allowed me to experience His love through my vision, and my soul had unequivocally responded to this unconditional and indescribably intense love, being radiated from Jesus, by wanting to die instantaneously just to be with Him for all eternity.

Although I had been religious throughout my lifetime and ever since I was about six years of age, I had always known, in my heart and soul, that God continuously played an extremely significant role in my life. And I can now honestly say, most confidently and without any doubt whatsoever, that my life is essentially meaningless without God.

And during the times in my life when my faith had wavered to an all-time low, I had noticed that I was angry with God; I had rejected Him, and I had actually believed that my life would improve dramatically if I were to exclude God from my life. But in actual fact, I only became more unhappy than ever before and terrified of life in general, as a direct consequence of this.

In addition, I still love God with all of my heart, mind, strength and soul, even after having been forced to endure so many difficult and, at times, unbearable trials and tribulations during my lifetime.

Consequently, I ask myself this very question: "How can I still love God so intensely, deeply, completely and above all things, even after the unbearable suffering that my life has entailed, and continues to entail on an ongoing and constant basis?"

And I have realized that the answer to this question is really quite simple, and relates exclusively to Jesus since God is Love. I have always been so drawn to God, even as a teenager, especially since God is drawing me to Him, just as the Catholic priest had once explained to me during one of our sessions.

And as a result, I have been unable to resist God's Call since I truly and genuinely love Him with all of my heart, with all of my mind, with all of my soul, with every single cell in my body, and with all of my strength.

But I can't help feeling so much remorse for having been so afraid to follow Jesus for all of these years due to my irrational fears, and the perceived suffering that I was totally convinced being a Disciple of Jesus would entail. But what I had previously failed to take into account was that Jesus had suffered during His Passion,

Crucifixion and Death on the Cross at the hands of mankind, for the forgiveness of our sins.

And a question that I often ask myself is that, "Do we, as Christians and God's People, really appreciate and fully understand the extent to which Jesus Christ, our Lord and God, suffered during His Passion and Crucifixion for the benefit of each and every single one of us, as mortals on this earth, so that we may gain eternal life in Heaven with Jesus?"

I believe that what really needs to be taken into consideration here is that Jesus suffered 5,480 wounds during His Passion and Crucifixion, for each one of us, whether we currently believe in God and are actually spiritual people or not. Jesus never abandons us when we need Him, and He loves all of us unconditionally and infinitely, even during the times that we may fail to believe in Him, reject Him and not reciprocate His love. Jesus does not give up on us, and always gives us multiple chances to repent and come back to Him throughout the course of our lives.

Looking back at my life, I have arrived at the realization that life is indeed extremely difficult, and a constant struggle. Life does contain many, if not an endless number of constant trials and tribulations, and an element of pain and suffering. And there is, without a doubt, much suffering around the world in so many different and various forms.

However, since Jesus Himself suffered 5,480 wounds during His Passion and Crucifixion, it's not surprising that life on Earth for us, as mere mortals, also entails a great deal of suffering.

In the past, there were even times in my life when I had honestly felt as though I had died but was 'resurrected from the dead' through Jesus Christ, our Lord and God, Who is the Light of our world. An example of this is a recent ultrasound of my armpits during a routine breast check-up which revealed that I had developed a tiny 4mm lymph node which was found in my left armpit. The radiologist, at the time, recommended that this lump be monitored, and that a repeat ultrasound be performed in six months' time. And after a period of six months had lapsed, the repeat ultrasound found the lymph node to be unchanged which was news that I truly welcomed at the time.

My life has encompassed countless challenges which I have always managed to overcome with continual prayer, faith, hope and trust in God.

And after suddenly arriving at a new revelation which almost took my breath away - the conclusion to this book – a most unexpected event occurred in my life. My faith suddenly took a turn for the worse, and I seriously began to doubt myself. This occurrence happened a short time after experiencing my most recent religious dream encompassing the light green crocodile and the physical sensation that I had felt whilst Jesus and St Michael the Archangel had held my hands.

I began to enter into a very dark place, and seriously considered turning away from God. I was absolutely terrified at the time, since abandoning God was the last thing that I had ever wanted or imagined that I would ever do, and I was stricken with fear and panic.

All of the negative events that had occurred in my life in the past began to consume my everyday thoughts and, once again, I questioned God's love for me. I simply couldn't understand how God could have allowed me to go to hospital over a year ago, against my will, and why I had had to endure so much constant and relentless suffering in my life.

I began to distance myself from God, and I built an emotional wall between us. I began to wonder if my life would have contained so much less suffering if I had not been such a pious person. I truly felt as though God had abandoned me, and had finally let me go.

I experienced extreme unhappiness during this period of time, and I was overwhelmed by feelings of great concern that I would never be able to regain my faith in God again. In my heart, I knew that turning away from God was the last thing that I would ever wish to do. But as each day passed, I distanced myself, more and more, from God and consequently, I became extremely unhappy, insecure and afraid of life in general, as a result.

In my heart and soul, I knew that I loved God - I had never doubted this fact - but what I was truly struggling to deal with at the time was that I simply couldn't understand why I was experiencing such negative thoughts about God, and why I was suddenly rehashing so many painful memories of my past life events which were, in essence, only serving the purpose of creating an even higher emotional wall between God and myself, when I had really wanted, more than anything, to be able to break this wall down again.

In desperation, I notified the Catholic priest and asked for his prayers since I had become so detached from God that I was now no longer able to pray for myself. Since I believed that this particular priest's prayers were extremely powerful, I truly felt that he would be able to help me more than anyone else, especially since, in my view, he was one of the most Holy priests that I had ever met in my entire life.

The next morning, when I awoke in bed, my immediate thoughts were solely about God. I truly missed Him, and I felt so much love for God. I prayed to Him with such fervour, and I begged God to always bring me back to Him if I were to ever stray from Jesus in the future. I prayed to God to help me become a pious person again, and it was apparent that all I had really needed at the time was some assistance in finding God again because I knew, deep in my heart and soul, that I could never truly live without God in my life.

After having entered into a very dark place, most unexpectedly and unwillingly, Jesus in all of His Glory, revealed His Light to me, like a beacon shining brightly in the night sky. And it was then that I realized that Jesus had, in fact, been holding my hand (as per my dream) throughout my darkest hour, and that Light had prevailed over darkness, once more.

As a family, we always attended Mass on Sundays whenever possible. And during Mass, one particular Sunday, I remember having the most incredible spiritual experience which I would like to take this opportunity to share with you now.

After receiving the Holy Eucharist, I suddenly began to feel an immense love for Jesus which caused me to become extremely emotional at the time. I immediately knew that He was allowing me to feel His love as a result of having received Jesus into my soul. Consequently, I gazed up at the large Cross of Jesus on the wall, situated behind the Altar, and I just couldn't help but feel such an intense love for Him which was so strong that my eyes began to water almost immediately. I quickly rubbed my eyes in an attempt to hide my tears to prevent any of the other parishioners in the congregation from noticing that I was crying during the Mass, and I now felt more content than ever before. I had so desperately felt the need to feel God's love again, especially since entering into a period of complete darkness a short while earlier, and after having seriously contemplated turning away from God due to my most painful past life events.

I had also, by now, at the age of 53 years, arrived at the extremely strong realization that during my lifetime, I was actually embarking on a spiritual journey to find Jesus. I had chosen to use the bridge (as per my dream) that Jesus had provided for me, for my own personal safety, rather than to swim in the water beneath it and risk drowning. I had been walking along this bridge, tenaciously and arduously, for all of my life. But notably, there were also times in my life in which I had experienced tremendous fear – a real fear of slipping off this bridge and landing in the water which would have inevitably led to my drowning.

Whilst in the process of stacking the dishwasher after breakfast, one morning, I happened to be feeling extremely unhappy at the time. My soul just felt so incredibly empty. And I honestly felt as though I desperately needed to feel the presence of Jesus in order to be able to feel happy again. It was as though my soul was longing to be with Jesus, and I was truly finding this experience most difficult to bear. I was even struggling to complete my daily chores. I liken my experience, at the time, to that of a plant, slowly shrivelling up as a result of having been deprived of water.

I thought about praying to Jesus at the time to help me, but I decided to firstly complete stacking the dishwasher instead, so that I would have more free time on my hands to pray to Him later.

All of a sudden, I felt the extremely strong presence of Jesus, completely surrounding me. But most unexpectedly, I was absolutely astonished when, for the first time in my entire life, I actually felt as though my soul was burning with fire. My soul had truly felt as though it was on fire from the warmth of the Sacred Heart of Jesus. I can liken this most unforgettable and unique experience to standing in front of a fireplace/heater on a cold day, and feeling the warmth being radiated from this source of heat directly onto your body.

My soul had actually felt the warmth of God's love through the Sacred Heart of Jesus. But in addition to feeling this tremendous warmth being radiated from Jesus, I also experienced a feeling of extreme peace, love and above all, comfort in my soul. And my soul continued to feel His warmth, peace, love and comfort for an extended period of time.

After completing my task in stacking the dishwasher, my husband summoned the family to go for our daily walk with the dogs. I distinctly remember waiting for my husband in the front garden, with our two children, since Sam was still indoors at the time, preparing to leave the house.

At this stage, my soul was still experiencing the warmth, love, peace and comfort as a result of the Sacred Heart of Jesus, but this feeling was so overwhelming that I suddenly felt as though I wanted to die instantaneously, just to be with Jesus. And it's of extreme importance to note here that this feeling of wanting to die to be with Jesus, was totally out of my control. I couldn't help but feel this way, and I didn't care about anything else at the time, during this particular spiritual experience.

But almost immediately after I had felt this way, I could actually feel my soul slowly becoming colder and colder until it had finally returned to its original and former self. And to help you understand exactly what I mean by this, I can liken my experience to standing in front of a fireplace/heater and enjoying the warmth that is being radiated from this heat source. But then, after suddenly moving away from the heat source, your body begins to feel cold again.

After experiencing the Sacred Heart of Jesus, I have arrived at the strong realization that my life is totally out of my control and as mentioned earlier in this book, nothing can happen in this world unless it's either the Ordained or Permitting Will of God since He is our Creator and Life-source.

There is no doubt in my mind whatsoever and in accordance with the Catholic Priest's sentiments, the reason why I am so drawn to God is because God is drawing me to Him. And in relation to my spiritual experience encompassing the Sacred Heart of Jesus and my wanting to die to be with Him, I would just like to emphasize most strongly here that this was definitely not a conscious decision that I had chosen to make at the time but was, in fact, beyond my control. I would never wish to die and leave my husband and children behind on this earth to fend for themselves without my ongoing help and spiritual guidance, because I adore them more than words can possibly express, and I want to be the best wife and mother that I can possibly be for them.

I would be most grateful to God if He were to allow me to live to a ripe old age as a mortal on this earth, so that I may spend as much quality time with my own family as possible. But when a mortal feels and experiences God's love to such a high degree, as I have been most blessed and privileged to be able to experience in my life, it's inevitable to wish to die to be with God in order to be able to continue to feel His infinite and unconditional love for all eternity. The intensity of God's love is far greater than mere words can ever hope to be able to express.

A while ago, whilst I was busily engaged in my daily chores, I suddenly felt such an intense love for my own personal Guardian Angel who had caused me to become rather emotional at the time, so much so, that my eyes actually began to water. And the only possible explanation that I had arrived at for having had this most beautiful spiritual experience was that my soul had responded to the love that my Guardian Angel had radiated to me at the time.

Recently, I experienced another vision, but this time, my vision encompassed my own Guardian Angel which gave me more of an insight into her true physical appearance. She has curly (as in ringlets), pale golden blonde, slightly past shoulder-length hair and a fringe which is not curly but instead, has a large wave embodied through it.

My Guardian Angel has large round blue eyes, and wears an extremely pale yellow dress consisting of a crew neckline which is lined with frills of the same coloured material. In addition, she has a thin waist and the hemline of the skirt of her dress is also lined with pale yellow frills of the same colour as her dress. Overall, my Guardian Angel is exceptionally pretty.

She also exhibits only one pair of pure white feathery wings unlike the Archangels.

I believe that a mistake that we may often make in life is that we forget that God has assigned each and every one of us with our own personal Guardian Angel to protect us, and who always remain with us until the day we die and pass from this life and into the next. And just because we are unable to visibly see God's most Holy Angels, doesn't mean that they don't exist, since they are always there, with us, to guide, protect and look after us. Angels are pure in soul and not only love God and each other, but also love the mortals that they have been assigned to look after on this earth.

I truly feel sorry for Guardian Angels because we, as mortals, may fail to acknowledge their existence since they are completely invisible to us. We may ignore, never pay much attention to them, fail to pray to our Guardian Angels, and be unappreciative of the special ways in which they always look after us, during our life journey.

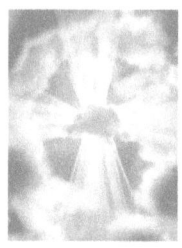

# CHAPTER 20

I soon experienced another vision but this time, it was of my husband's own personal Guardian Angel. Sam's Guardian Angel has extremely short black curly hair and blue eyes. He has dark skin tones and a muscular physique. He actually wears bright red shorts, has a muscly chest and very large muscles on his arms. But it's of great importance to make the distinction here that although his muscles are large, they are not as immense in size and magnitude as the muscles belonging to the Archangels in comparison.

My husband's personal Guardian Angel has only one pair of pure white feathery wings which are exactly the same shape as that of my own Guardian Angel's wings. He has a bare chest and his wings are actually embedded into his back.

Sam recently recited an event to me which involved a true account of a freak incident that occurred whilst he was driving by himself, one day, along a busy freeway, before we met. My husband suddenly saw a car tyre rolling towards his car, hit the guard rail and then bounce over the windscreen of his car. At the time, Sam thought that he was very lucky that the car tyre didn't actually fly straight through his windscreen which could have resulted in the most dire and catastrophic consequences for Sam.

I immediately informed my husband that, in my view, there is no such thing as luck in life. But instead, his own personal Guardian Angel had saved his life that day and had protected him from potentially being involved in a car accident which could have led to his death, especially if the car tyre had directly hit the windscreen of Sam's car at full force.

And it's of the utmost importance here to remember that our Guardian Angels are always with us, by our side, protecting and looking after us, even though we are unable to see them in their physical form.

Our Guardian Angels are also considerably physically stronger than we are, as mere mortals, and so our Guardian Angels can save us in any given situation in order to protect us from harm, in accordance with God's Will.

I have always retained a very strong belief in God and in His existence even before I began to experience visions, religious dreams and other spiritual experiences. However, admittedly, there have been times in my life when I was angry with God as a result of having been unable to bear my life circumstances at the time, and for being pushed beyond my threshold for tolerance for pain and suffering.

Most ashamedly and regretfully, there have also been times in my life when I had actually said out loud to my family that I didn't believe in God because I had strongly felt, at the time, that my suffering was too great for me to be able to continue to bear. But immediately afterwards, I knew, in my heart and soul, that I was blatantly lying to myself, and to my family.

During these times, I was absolutely terrified of God, especially since I had always retained such a holy fear of Him, and I became extremely afraid that God would punish me for saying such a sinful and offensive remark in the presence of God.

I now strongly believe that God doesn't actually punish people on this earth but rather, His intention is purely to try to save every single mortal's soul from the Fires of Hell. And in this way, we are all given the opportunity to attain the highest privilege and honour in being able to spend all eternity with God in Heaven after we die.

God always gives us multiple chances to repent in life, and to build on the Grace that Jesus granted each and every one of us as a result of His Passion, Death on the Cross and Resurrection, through Baptism. But ultimately, when our life, as mortals, comes to an end, we must all stand before God on Judgement Day and face the consequences of our actions. And during this time, we are at God's mercy and it's our Creator Who ultimately decides if the deeds performed by each mortal on this earth, warrants our admission to Heaven, Purgatory or Hell.

I would now like to share one of my favourite prayers that I found in a prayer book and it reads: "Do not believe in chance but learn to see the Hand of God, Your Father Who loves you, in everything that happens." And I believe this prayer to be true, without a doubt.

I was busy vacuuming, one afternoon, when I suddenly felt such an intense love towards Our Lady which made me rather teary and emotional at the time. And this spiritual experience caused me to think about my dream encompassing the Immaculate Virgin Mary when I had failed to tell the Mother of God that I loved Her. And even to this day, after a period of about eight years has passed, I still wish, with all of my heart, that I had told Our Lady how much I truly loved Her, in my dream, since it was the perfect opportunity to be able to convey this to Her in person.

But I would like to strongly emphasize at this point that it was actually my intense love for the Mother of God that led me back to Her after my sibling had initially called me away from the Immaculate Virgin Mary in my dream. Nevertheless, I will still always regret and feel sad that I missed this great and once in a lifetime opportunity to tell Our Lady how much I truly loved Her at the time, and always will.

After having rehashed some very painful memories from my past whilst writing this autobiography, I found myself becoming most upset over the past two days at having given away the Cross of Jesus to my sibling that I had found lying in the gutter, one rainy and dreary day, a number of years ago now.

I treasured this Crucifix of Jesus with all of my heart, and this Cross was extremely precious to me. As a result, I was now experiencing tremendous remorse for having given away this Cross of Jesus, as a special gift to Penelope in the past.

But most unexpectedly, I experienced yet another vision during the night, which actually helped me to overcome my extreme feelings of guilt for having given away this Crucifix of Jesus to my sibling.

Although it was another vision of Jesus on the Cross, it was most unlike my previous vision that I had witnessed over a year ago of the Crucifix of Jesus in the Flesh which was life-sized and allowed me to experience God's love so intensely that I had wished to die instantaneously just to be with Him.

In my most recent vision, the Crucifix of Jesus was made of metal, and was similar to the type of Crucifix that you would find attached to a Rosary, although much larger in size. But what took me by surprise in this vision was that the Cross of Jesus was actually leaning forwards, towards me, which I believe is of great significance. The interpretation that I have been enlightened with regarding the Crucifix of Jesus leaning forwards in my vision is that God would like me to finally lay my past to rest, so as to enable me to be able to focus solely on the present and future, as a result.

When I awoke, I felt really startled as I often feel after experiencing visions during the night. But afterwards, I arrived at the really strong realisation that my sibling truly loves the Cross of Jesus that I had given her as a gift, and that I should never ask Penelope to return it to me under any circumstances.

After my vision, I quickly realized that Penelope may currently have in her possession the most beautiful and extremely precious Cross of Jesus that I had found lying in the gutter, but I was the one who was blessed with being given the rarest opportunity in being able to experience God's love through my vision of the Crucifix of Jesus over a year ago now. And no one can ever take that away from me.

Therefore, my vision of Jesus on the Cross, leaning forwards, was a clear sign that I needed to leave all of the suffering that I had experienced in my past behind me, and that it was of the utmost importance that I focus on the present and in making my future, as bright as it can possibly be.

I knew that, deep in my heart and soul, I could never live without God as being a part of my life because Jesus truly loves me unconditionally and infinitely; God never forces me to do anything that I do not wish to do; He is constantly there for me whenever I need Him the most; Jesus is always patient with me, and He continuously gives me multiple chances to repent and come back to Him without ever forcing me to do this.

I chose to come back to God and to become a Disciple of Jesus through my own freewill, because I love God above all things in my life and so intensely, with all of my heart, with all of my soul, with all of my mind and with all of my strength.

And it suddenly dawned on me that I had grown to love God, over time, in a similar way to which I love my own family – namely my husband and children – but far more intensely, however, and above all things in my life.

At this stage in my life, I was exceptionally happy, and I had never felt as spiritually close to Jesus as I had become at this point in time.

I have also arrived at the strong realization that since God is Love, everything that He does for me is for the sanctification and salvation of my soul, and is always in my own best interests.

And I will always feel so much gratitude towards this extremely special Catholic priest for assisting me to be able to see my life situation as it truly was and for his spiritual guidance, help and belief in me at the time.

# CHAPTER 21

After experiencing another period of darkness, I suddenly felt the strong presence of Jesus Christ and most unexpectedly, I experienced a vision of the Head and Face of Jesus. And this was the first time in my life that I had ever experienced a vision of the Risen Lord.

I strongly believed that Jesus was enabling me to realize that I wasn't alone in my suffering, and that He was always with me, even during the times that I felt that I was alone. Jesus gave me the strength that I had so desperately needed at the time to be able to bear the unbearable, and to acquire the determination and courage to overcome my extreme emotional torment and torture.

And after retiring to bed for the evening, whilst praying to St Michael the Archangel, I suddenly received reassurance that Jesus still loved me by experiencing one of the largest Holy Spirit Touches that I had ever received before from Jesus.

Three days after experiencing my initial vision comprising the Head and Face of Jesus, I suddenly experienced another vision which encompassed the Body of Jesus Who wore a brilliant white garment, and His outstretched arms were inviting me to come to Him so that Jesus could comfort me during my time of need.

In essence, Jesus Christ saved me during my darkest hour since Jesus heals all wounds. I soon realized that only Jesus was truly capable of 'resurrecting me from the dead' and was solely responsible for mending and healing the excruciating pain and suffering that I was experiencing at the time.

The very next day, whilst praying earnestly with my eyes closed, to Jesus on my knees, in front of my beautiful statue of Our Lady holding Baby Jesus in Her arms, I suddenly experienced a crystal clear vision. In the vision, I saw a large opening in Heaven encompassing the most realistic looking white fluffy clouds which were slowly moving across the sky at the time. And although I couldn't actually physically see a gate, I immediately knew that I was witnessing the Gateway to Heaven.

I would like to strongly emphasize, at this point in time, that I was considerably shocked when I experienced this vision since it was totally unexpected and I was most unaware of its meaning. Whilst standing outside the Gate, I had especially noticed that it was so peaceful, quiet and serene in Heaven. I had also inferred Heaven to be a really vast and infinitely large open area which seemed to have no end in sight.

And my vision of the Gateway to Heaven is verification for the true existence of Heaven. I strongly believe that the reason why I had experienced this vision is symbolic of the fact that I have now chosen to follow the right path in life, the path of righteousness. I truly felt that God had assisted me to get back on track to my original path which I had chosen to follow.

I soon came to realize that I was, in fact, most able to manage and overcome life's constant challenges, with the unfailing help of Jesus Christ, our Lord and God. And as a result of all of my spiritual experiences to date, I have also arrived at the strong realization that mortals have failed to be able to help me in the way that only God could. Jesus has always been able to assist me to feel happy again, even during the times when I was feeling particularly despondent and melancholy; alleviate my extreme emotional pain and suffering; continually be there for me, every minute of every day and most importantly, Jesus has never abandoned me during my time of need in the way that mortals have in the past.

So, in summary, as a direct result of my religious experiences and close spiritual relationship with God, I have come to realize that I am never truly alone in life since Jesus is always with me. He provides me with His great comfort and continual assistance which, in turn, has enabled me to be able to overcome each and every obstacle, trial and tribulation that I was most suddenly and unexpectedly confronted with during my lifetime.

I have also arrived at the extremely strong realization that I need Jesus to be a most integral part and the centre of my life, just as I need air to breathe. I require Jesus to be with me continually, to help me in my daily life and to alleviate my constant pain and suffering, in order to be able to experience true happiness in life.

Although Jesus has always been the Light of my life, my tremendous suffering in life had detracted me from the path of righteousness and was leading me down the path of destruction instead.

Recently, I experienced a most unexpected dream which involved my mother and sibling. In my dream, I was standing in a shoe shop, which was located in a large shopping centre, with my mother and sibling. My mother was proudly informing me of a really big discount that my sibling had received, for a particular purchase, due to her own merit. My mother had also mentioned, in a rather matter-of-fact manner, that Penelope wanted everyone to adore her.

I felt most perturbed at hearing my mother discuss Penelope in this way and I saw my sibling talking to a group of women, but she failed to acknowledge or even notice my presence. So, leaving my mother and sibling behind, I walked through a glass sliding door which led me to go outside the shopping centre. I had only walked a short distance before I encountered a dirt track alongside some trees, ahead of me, and what appeared to be open bushland. Overwhelming feelings of fear, being isolated, lost and alone suddenly overshadowed me. In a state of panic, I quickly turned back the way I had come. And finding the same door through which I had initially exited, I quickly re-entered the shopping centre. I soon found another door which also led me outside, only directly to my husband, this time. And the words, "adore her" kept swirling around in my mind, until I suddenly awoke and told Sam all about my dream.

Before long, I had arrived at the strong realization that my dream was actually a reflection of my life at the time. I had suddenly lost my identity, just as my recent dream had prophesied. Previously, I was unable to make my own decisions in life due to pressure from extended family members.

At the age of fifty-two, I was trapped in a body in which I was suddenly being forced to rediscover who I actually was as a person, in order to be able to find my true identity. And this was a new dilemma in my life which I now had to face on a daily basis, and that I struggled with immensely for a lengthy period of time.

I had also decided that I needed to become more independent and be given the opportunity to make my own decisions and mistakes in life.

So, after experiencing countless visions, religious dreams and spiritual experiences, I asked myself a most fundamental question which had been plaguing me for most of my life as a mortal on this earth. And the question that I have found myself asking, over and over again, is this: "What is the true meaning of life?"

Adam and Eve betrayed God by falling into snares set by Satan, in the Garden of Eden and consequently, they were ejected from Paradise which was closed afterwards, as a direct result of their grave sins.

In order to make atonement for the sins committed by Adam and Eve and all of mankind, Jesus suffered 5,480 wounds through His Passion and Crucifixion, rising from the dead on the third day, and reopening Heaven, as a result.

In Baptism, Jesus has made atonement for the sins of our parents through the Body and Blood of Christ. And during our lifetime, the responsibility lies with each and every one of us, as mortals, to build on the Grace that Jesus has already bestowed upon us through Baptism.

Contrary to the belief of many, we are not placed on this earth for our own selfish needs and desires. But instead, it's essential that we build up as much Grace as possible, throughout our lives, from Baptism all the way until Judgment Day.

During our lifetime, we are called, by God, to observe the Commandments set by Jesus which are to love God with all of our heart, with all of our soul and with all of our mind, as well as to love our neighbour as ourselves. And since Jesus Christ suffered in His Passion and Crucifixion, we too, must carry our own Cross for our Lord in order to become a Disciple of Jesus. And whether we believe in God or not, life does contain much suffering regardless of our beliefs. But it is of the utmost importance here to acknowledge the fact that for those mortals who believe in Our Lord and God, their suffering on Earth can and will be alleviated through the Body and Blood of Christ.

However, for those who fail to believe in the existence of Jesus Christ, the Only Begotten Son of Our Lord and God, Who is Seated at the Right Hand of the Father, and Whom God will send, at the End of the World, to judge the living and the dead, will suffer immeasurably due to the faith and trust that these mortals have placed in Satan Himself, who will take great pleasure in taunting and torturing these souls in Hell infinitively and for all eternity. These souls will inevitably beg God for the forgiveness of their sins, and to be relieved of their excruciating pain and suffering that the Devil relentlessly inflicts upon them. But their cries for help will not be heard since they themselves, failed to repent and hear God's Call whilst they were still mortals on this earth. Jesus always gives us multiple chances to repent for our sins in life so that when we become deceased and pass from this life and into the next, we may experience eternal life with our Lord and God in Heaven.

Recently, I experienced another vision, only this time, my vision encompassed a beautiful old-fashioned looking wooden door which displayed a number of decorative panels across it. The door suddenly opened in front of me. But although the door was only slightly ajar, however, I could actually still see through the slight opening. I saw some greenery, and something that appeared to look like a pasture containing green grass and trees. I tried to open this door to a larger extent since the scenery was most appealing to me, but the door just wouldn't budge. And after having received a revelation, I have realized that this door actually leads to the Era of Peace.

One night, a short while later, I experienced a vision of a brown, modern style door which suddenly swung open, to a large extent, in front of me but I could not make out what was actually behind this door since my line of vision was obscured, and extremely blurry. This particular door, also displayed a round metal brown handle to match the door's appearance in my vision. And after having received a recent revelation, I have since realized that this door leads to the Three Days of Darkness and to Hell itself.

And the reason why the door leading to the Three Days of Darkness swung open so readily and widely in comparison to the door leading to the Era of Peace is because more than three-quarters of the current population will be lost during the Three Days of Darkness, and these mortals shall not enter into the Era of Peace.

But the door leading to the Era of Peace, which was only slightly ajar, signifies the few reserved mortals who shall not perish during the Three Days of Darkness and will enter into the Era of Peace.

All of the mortals who have received the seal of God's Favour on their foreheads will not be terminated during the Three Days of

Darkness, and will be able to resume their life journey in the Era of Peace.

Recently, I experienced a vision of Satan and was given more of an insight into his true physical appearance. Satan is a complete skeleton and a portion of his fingers display raw red wounds which have resulted from being thrown into the furnace by Prince St Michael during the great angelic battle in Heaven. He has red glowing sunken eye sockets, two red horns on his skeletal head and black teeth. Since Satan Himself is a fallen Guardian Angel, his wings are the same shape as that of Guardian Angels but are black in colour.

For so many years, I had distanced myself from Jesus Christ as as a result of being afraid to follow Him which had prevented me from becoming a Disciple of Jesus. But now, I have arrived at the strong realization that Jesus has always helped and been there for me through all of my trials and tribulations in life, despite the fact that I had turned my back on Him.

And we must never lose sight of the fact that Satan and his demons will most relentlessly, always try to take us away from God at every opportunity.

Therefore, it is of the utmost importance that we pray fervently to St Michael the Archangel, who is Prince of the Nine Choirs of Angels and the Leader of God's Heavenly Hosts, for his continual protection from the Enemy and to assist us to recognize the constant snares that Satan relentlessly sets before us in order to detain and detract mortals from following the path of righteousness. And by praying to St Michael the Archangel on a daily basis, he will be responsible for leading us to God, so that our souls may experience the burning flame of God's love, both on Earth and in the Kingdom of Heaven, for all eternity.

Our true and final destinations are accomplished in life only after our souls have been lifted from our bodies and we pass from this life and into the next. And depending on whether we performed holy or evil deeds as mortals, our souls will either go straight to Heaven if we were living Saints during our life on Earth; go to Purgatory first and then progress to Heaven once our souls have been purified, or go straight to Hell and remain there infinitively to be taunted and tortured by Satan relentlessly and for all eternity.

By following Jesus, in loving Him with all of our heart, mind, strength and soul, and by trying our utmost to obey His Holy Commandments, Jesus will lead us along the path of righteousness and help us to live our lives according to the Way, the Truth and the Life in which case He will prepare a place for us in Heaven so that we may enjoy the fruits of our labours in the afterlife.

And to expect our lives not to contain any form of suffering whatsoever but to only ever experience peace and happiness instead, is a fairy tale in itself, and would be a most unrealistic expectation incapable of ever being fulfilled since Jesus, Who is God Himself, suffered 5,480 wounds through His Passion and Crucifixion.

Life on Earth is a constant struggle, and does contain much suffering which is evident in so many different forms around the world. But a key element that should always be taken into consideration is that only Jesus, Who is God Himself and our only True and Living God, is capable of alleviating and eliminating our great suffering on Earth.

My spiritual experiences encompassing Jesus are real. God's love is real, unconditional and infinite. And in my 53 years of existence, I have finally come to realize that God has continued to love me even during the times that I had turned away from Him; had failed to reciprocate His love, and had even falsely renounced His existence.

During my life, God has always been so infinitely patient with me. He has helped me to overcome each and every single one of my trials and tribulations; He has never forced me to do anything that I was reluctant to do; Jesus never forced me to take up my Cross and follow Him; God never forced me to do His Will, and He never forced me to do things that were not in my own best interests.

God invites every mortal on this earth to follow Jesus, and to become a Disciple of His. But as a direct result of the freewill that God has bestowed upon each one of us from birth, He never forces us to do this. Instead, God would like mortals to fight for Him and to come to Jesus through our own freewill, and not because He is forcing us to love and be obedient to Him.

In my dream encompassing the Apparition of Our Lady, the Mother of God, that I experienced eight years ago now, my sibling had called me away from the Immaculate Virgin Mary, and I had most reluctantly left Her to join Penelope who had believed that the clouds in the sky looked so beautiful. However, in my view, the clouds actually looked fake, and were not real. But since then, I have come to realize that this part of my dream was a prophecy in predicting the series of events which would occur in my life, involving my sibling, after a period of six years had passed.

After becoming so spiritually close to God through countless spiritual experiences including my many visions, religious dreams and supernatural encounters, I have arrived at the extremely strong realization that God is Real, as is Jesus, Our Lady, St Michael the Archangel, the seven Archangels who stand before the Throne of God, Guardian Angels, Heaven, Hell and Satan.

Recently, I experienced two new visions of the Archangels, St Raphael and St Gabriel:

St Raphael the Healer has two pairs of pure white feathery wings. One pair of his wings point upwards towards Heaven, whilst the other pair point downwards towards Hell.

Although his wings are of a similar shape to that of St Michael the Archangel's, his wing span is not of the same magnitude as Prince St Michael's.

St Raphael the Healer has black curly hair with deep blue eyes which resemble the colour of the ocean. He is extremely muscular in physique, and is only slightly shorter than Prince St Michael in stature. On each arm, he wears a golden cuff with an engraved inscription which reads: "St Raphael the Healer", since this magnificent Archangel is also a Healing Angel.

St Raphael the Healer wears gold tunic armour which is similar in appearance to that of Prince St Michael's and on his feet, he wears long brown Roman sandals.

St Gabriel the Archangel, on the other hand, has three pairs of pure white feathery wings which are also of a similar shape to that of Prince St Michael.

His top pair of wings point upwards towards Heaven whilst his middle pair of wings point downwards towards Earth. St Gabriel the Archangel's bottom pair of wings neatly wrap around and cover his feet. And on his feet, he wears long brown Roman sandals similar to those worn by St Raphael the Healer.

On each arm, he also wears a golden cuff with an engraved inscription which reads: "St Gabriel Archangel".

Whilst editing my autobiography, I suddenly experienced a vision of St Gabriel Archangel's hair and face. He has brown eyes and light brown/blonde hair which just touches his shoulders. Although his hair is straight, it contains long layers which gives the appearance of his hair exuberating much body and volume. St Gabriel Archangel has a thick fringe containing long strands of hair, and his hairstyle also promotes the appearance of hair being blown in the wind.

God invites each of us, as mortals on this earth, to include Him in our everyday lives and to pray constantly to God so that we may walk with Jesus along the path of righteousness in our journey through life.

It's God's Will that we come to Him and love God through our own freewill, and of our own choosing. Jesus is infinitely patient with each and every one of us, and He gives us multiple chances to repent and come back to Him even during the times that we may have strayed. Our Lord is constantly there for us whenever we need Him, and God will always open the door to us whenever we decide to knock on His door.

By reflecting on my past, it recently dawned on me that Jesus was always there for me, assisting me to overcome all of my trials and tribulations in life. And when we turn to Jesus, we are essentially placing all of our faith and trust in Him. God will guide, protect and help us continuously and unfailingly throughout our entire existence as mortals on this earth; Jesus will never disappoint us.

I have always believed and known, in my heart and soul, that I was never psychotic. God would never have allowed a Mystic like myself to ever become psychotic, especially when taking into consideration the countless visions, religious dreams and supernatural encounters that I continue to experience on a regular basis.

When I turned to God to the extreme, over a year ago, it was an act of mercy from Jesus. God saved me from following the path of destruction, and Jesus allowed me to become as spiritually close to Him as I had so desperately craved to be for my entire life, as a result.

The only way that I was able to cope with my current life circumstances at the time of my forced hospital admission was to turn to God to the extreme and through God's Mysteries, Jesus had essentially instigated the help that I had needed in order for the sun to be able to shine through the clouds. Again, God had come to my aid, and saved me during my darkest hour. Jesus lifted the fog that had engulfed my life for more than 52 years of my existence, and I was now in a position to be able to decipher Light from darkness, the truth from lies and deceit, and live my life according to the Way, the Truth and the Life.

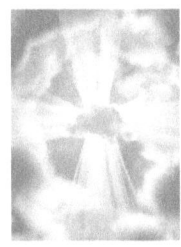

# CHAPTER 22

I realized that what I now needed to do in my life, more than anything else, was to learn to place all of my faith and trust in Jesus, our Lord and God.

But how can we actually learn to do this if we fail to fully understand exactly what it means to have faith in God?

And in answer to this question, I have arrived at the strong realization that faith is hope. By possessing faith, we believe with all of our heart, with all of our mind, with all of our soul and with all of our strength, that our prayers and petitions to God will be answered if we continue to retain hope and if we believe, without a doubt, that nothing is impossible through God.

So, if faith is hope, then what is the spiritual definition of trust? How can we actually learn to place all of our trust in our Resurrected Lord, Jesus Christ, the Light of our world?

If we are able to place all of our trust in God, consequently, we are being released from all of our inhibitions and fears in life, as a result.

Jesus is loyal and loves each and every one of us unconditionally, infinitively, and with a burning charity. Our Lord and God can always be trusted because Jesus is the Way, the Truth and the Life. The Saviour of our world always has our own best interests at heart, and the suffering that we endure on Earth is for the sanctification and purification of our soul so that we may enjoy eternal life with God in Heaven in the afterlife.

For my entire adult life, I was consumed by an extreme fear of the unknown, and of the great suffering and torment that tomorrow may bring. Recently, however, I have realized that fear always comes from Satan and not from God. But if we pray to St Michael the Archangel on a daily basis, he will alleviate our fears, and be responsible for bringing us spiritually closer to God since it's always the Enemy who tries his utmost to take us away from God.

However, it's of crucial importance to be able to make a distinction between possessing a holy fear of God and having an irrational fear of the unknown and of future events that may occur in our lives.

By retaining a holy fear of God, we are acknowledging God's existence, His infinite power and strength, and His ability to achieve the impossible in life. But by experiencing a constant fear of what the future may bring, we are expressing a lack of faith and trust in God.

And I now believe, without a doubt, that Jesus loves me. He has shown, and allowed me to feel His love many times throughout my life in the form of visions, religious dreams and spiritual experiences. I also acknowledge that Jesus loves each and every one of us including those who do not reciprocate His love.

By choosing to follow Jesus, Who is the Way, the Truth and the Life, through our own freewill, we no longer need to fear life itself, nor what the future may bring for us, since it's always God's intention to save every single mortal's soul on this earth.

Recently, I was made privy to witnessing the Gateway to Heaven through a vision that I experienced. I am most blessed to have received verification that Heaven truly does exist. When Jesus was crucified on the Cross, He reopened the Gateway to Heaven by rising from the dead. And in doing so, Jesus has bestowed upon us, the greatest honour and privilege of being able to experience immortality after we die, so that we can continue to live for all eternity with our Lord and God in Heaven.

And if we pray to St Michael the Archangel on a daily basis, he will not only bring us spiritually closer to God, but St Michael the Archangel will also help us to identify and avoid the snares that the Enemy constantly and relentlessly sets before each and every one of us in an attempt to detract us from the path of righteousness.

If we allow Satan to take us down the path of destruction, then the Enemy and/or his demons can have partial/complete control of the souls that he inhabits to ensure that he is able to taunt and torture these souls in Hell infinitively and for all eternity as a result of the deadly sins that they have committed as mortals on this earth.

However, if we choose to become a Disciple of Jesus, as a result of our own freewill, we can be assured that Jesus will prepare a place for us in Heaven; we will fail to live in fear of what tomorrow may bring, and throughout all of our trials and tribulations in life, Jesus will always be there for us; He will never abandon us, and our Lord will continually alleviate our pain and suffering during our time of need.

And I have come to realize that there is no way in this world that I would have been able to become as spiritually close to Jesus, as I am today, if it were not for St Michael the Archangel's constant help and intercession in keeping the Enemy and Liar at bay.

In re-addressing my question about the need to display trust in God, the key in being able to achieve this most important component of the Roman Catholic religion is St Michael the Archangel. By directing our prayers to Prince St Michael and in asking him for his constant intercession, he will inevitably bring us spiritually closer to God, and will assist us to identify the traps that Satan relentlessly sets before us in an attempt to detract us from the Way, the Truth and the Life.

By placing all of our trust in God, we are essentially allowing Jesus to take full control of our lives rather than the Enemy who continuously attempts to do this, unbeknown to us, as mortals. It's a known fact that Satan never has our best interests at heart; he hates us with a passion.

Satan desires to inflict the most excruciatingly unbearable events and circumstances upon each and every one of us on a daily basis. And as a direct consequence of this, our souls will experience intolerable torture, torment, unrest and the most unimaginable anguish, pain and suffering possible.

When we ask God, as a result of our own freewill, to take full control of our lives, as I have done, we are essentially placing all of our faith and trust in God. And in doing so, we are failing to allow Satan to take partial/full control of our lives instead, and we have given God our permission to take care of us in the way that He sees fit, so that we may enter into God's Kingdom when our time on this earth finally comes to an end.

I asked God, through prayer, to take full control of my life since I knew, in my heart and soul, that God truly loves me unconditionally and infinitely, even with all of my shortcomings. God always has my own best interests at heart; He never abandons me during my time of need; Jesus always helps me to successfully overcome all of my trials and tribulations in life, and only God has the true ability to grant me the love, comfort, peace, tranquillity, happiness and joy that my own soul craves to experience so desperately as a mortal on this earth.

Satan creates doubt in our intellect, and prevents mortals from becoming spiritually close to God. By choosing to take up our own Cross, through our own freewill, in order to follow Jesus, Satan loses control over us, and is therefore unable to taunt and torture our souls in Hell for all eternity.

Every negative thought and display of human behaviour is a direct consequence of the Enemy's influence. However, every positive thought and display of human behaviour comes from God.

People that we know, and have met over the course of our lives, always have the ability to let us down, reject us, break our hearts, hurt us more deeply than words can ever possibly express, disappoint us, make us feel as though we are truly insignificant and worthless human beings on this earth, and even abandon us during our time of need.

But Jesus, on the other hand, always has our own best interests at heart. And I would like to reiterate that He wishes to save each and every one of us, as mortals, and our Lord will never abandon us during our time of need. Jesus is always there for us, even during the times that we may think that He has abandoned us. God always gives us multiple chances to repent, and to turn back to Him even after we have strayed.

And it's of crucial importance to emphasize that God loves each and every one of us unconditionally and with a burning charity. And even during the times that we may feel unloved by others, isolated, alone, rejected by society in general or even by our loved ones, we are never truly alone in this world since God is always with us continually, and He will never reject us when we turn to Him for help.

Therefore, we should never feel alone during the times that we may believe that the entire world is against us, because God will continually be there for us, even when no one else will. We can always trust God fully and completely, since He is our Creator and loves us more than anyone else in this world ever could.

Jesus Christ, God's Only Begotten Son, was sent by His Father, our Lord and God, to make atonement for the sins of mankind. From Baptism, the onus is on our godparents to ensure that we are raised in a most holy and spiritual environment. However, this responsibility is transferrable, and rests solely on our own shoulders throughout adulthood. It is of crucial importance that during our lives as mortals on this earth, we build on the Grace that Jesus has so gloriously bestowed upon us as a result of the Crucified Body and Blood of Christ.

But in relation to those mortals who have diminished or completely lost God's Favour, they must stand trial before God on Judgement Day, and face the consequences of their actions. Mortals such as these, inherit the risks associated with the most severe form of retribution which involves spending all eternity in Hell with no possibility of being granted a reprieve.

Being a most pious and spiritual mortal on this earth, God has blessed me with gifts that I consider to be priceless in value, and for which no amount of money could ever hope to purchase – namely my husband and two children. In addition, God has bestowed upon me the highest privilege and honour of being able to experience visions, religious dreams and spiritual experiences which consequently led to my becoming spiritually closer to Jesus, as a result.

A most important revelation which was bestowed upon me only recently regarding God's love for His People on Earth is that God exhibits no favourites, nor does Jesus reward one good deed over another based on the particular status of the mortal in question. All good deeds, performed by mortals, are rewarded according to their merit.

In relation to mortals who have either rejected or fail to believe in God, good deeds performed by these individuals are rewarded by Jesus in the form of consolations involving riches/material possessions on Earth.

Alternatively, for those mortals who exhibit a belief in God, and who love Jesus with all of their heart, soul, mind and body, theirs is the Kingdom of Heaven and they shall receive their reward in the afterlife, as well as on Earth.

Since early childhood, I have always possessed an extremely holy fear of God. For years, I believed that God punished mortals for their sins on Earth. But I can now state with complete conviction that my assumptions about God were completely unsubstantiated and false.

# CHAPTER 23

God loves each and every one of us more than the human brain can ever possibly comprehend and understand. It pleases God when we ask Jesus for His help. If we knock on God's door, it shall be opened to us; if we seek Jesus, we shall find Him. And during the times that we may have forsaken God, He patiently awaits our return.

But it's of the utmost importance to always remember that Jesus continues to love His People with a burning charity, even during the times that we may fail to reciprocate God's love.

As mere mortals on this earth, we may not always understand why God allows certain things to happen, both in the world and in our own lives.

A sudden occurrence of a bad turn of events in our lives may cause us to experience an element of unrest, anxiety, grief, melancholy, and/or fear in our souls. And as mortals, we may even be tempted to turn away from God, as a result, and believe that God is punishing us when, in fact, the opposite is true. But it's of the utmost importance here to note that in these circumstances, Jesus is actually helping in the salvation of our souls. As mortals, however, we are only able to see the smaller picture but God, Who is the Creator and Saviour of our World, is always able to see the bigger picture and hence, these are a part of God's Mysteries.

Only recently, I actually felt as though I was able to become my true self, and that I could leave my old self behind. I was finally given the freedom to decipher where my life was heading; experience true happiness in life; follow my own dreams, and become the person that I had always wanted to be in life.

Furthermore, I was now able to emerge from the thick and hazy fog which had enveloped my life from childhood until middle age which, in turn, enabled me to be able to follow the path of righteousness, through my own freewill.

And in following Jesus (the Truth), whom I have grown, over time, to absolutely love and adore more intensely than words can ever possibly hope to express, I am now able to serve my Lord and God and devote the rest of my life, as a mortal on this earth, in being a Disciple of Jesus. And as a direct consequence of this, I have become spiritually closer to Him, as a result, since Jesus is the Way, the Truth and the Life.

At this point in time, I strongly felt compelled to put my past behind me to the very best of my ability, and to concentrate more on the present and future, which would allow me to be able to focus on the special blessings that God has graciously bestowed upon me, namely my wonderful husband, who is my soulmate and best friend, as well as my two beautiful children.

So, in a nutshell, I can never hope to deny the fact that life is extremely difficult, and always does contain a certain element of pain and suffering. Admittedly, sometimes our suffering may even reach unbearable and intolerable levels. But it's of crucial importance here to strongly emphasize that Jesus, Who is God Himself, suffered during His Passion and Crucifixion for each and every one of us so that we may spend eternal life with God in Heaven in the afterlife.

God has given us the freewill to either choose to follow Jesus or fail to allow God to be involved in our lives. But it's of crucial importance here to understand that if we, as mortals, choose the latter option, we are essentially placing our lives in the hands of Satan, in which case we will be forced to constantly have to rely solely on ourselves when bad events occur, since we will no longer experience God's protection against all evil, as a direct consequence of having rejected Jesus.

But it's also of the utmost importance to always remember that God never forces us to include Him in our daily lives but rather, He extends an invitation to each and every one of us to take up our own Cross and follow Jesus. God always gives us the freewill to do as we please on this earth, and to make our own personal life choices.

However, since I am an extremely pious person, I feel most compelled to become as obedient to God as is humanly possible as a result of my gratitude for all of the blessings that Jesus has bestowed upon me in my life, and due to the fact that I genuinely love God above all things in this world.

As a Disciple of Jesus, God never forces me to do anything against my will. Through my own freewill, I have chosen to follow Jesus; both include and allow God to play a most significant role in my everyday life, and accomplish the missions that God has assigned me in order to fulfil His Will.

Since arriving at the realization that we are never truly alone in this world, I strongly believe that Jesus is always travelling with us during our journey in life. But the onus is on each and every one of us to ask for God's help during all of our trials and tribulations, since Jesus will never force us to do anything that we do not wish to do, due to the freewill that God has assigned each one of us from birth.

It's God's Will that we turn to Jesus during our time of need in life. God will never turn away those who come to Him, and earnestly ask for His assistance. And as mere mortals on this earth, we should always take heart in the knowledge that we are all God's People, irrespective of our race, heritage, financial position, status in life, occupation, and religious or cultural beliefs.

If we walk by faith, we can take great comfort in the fact that Jesus will hold our hand throughout our most difficult trials and tribulations in life. Consequently, God will also lighten our burden, as well as alleviate our pain and suffering in life. And as a result of God's infinite mercy, Jesus graciously grants us the fortitude needed in order to be able to successfully overcome the difficulties that continually envelop our lives.

Since we view and comprehend the world in accordance with our mortal human brains, we must constantly remind ourselves that God created the world in which we live, and everything that occurs is a direct consequence of either God's Ordained or His Permitting Will.

Jesus is my rock, as is St Michael the Archangel. Only recently, I arrived at the strong realization that Jesus has always been there for me, even during the times that I had felt totally alone in this world.

God is always with us, during both the good and bad times in our lives. Jesus is always there for us, holding our hand, during our times of pain and suffering in life. God loves us most unconditionally and infinitely, even during the times when we may feel that nobody else does.

Jesus will never leave us, nor will He ever abandon us, unlike mortals who have the potential to do this to us, over and over again, during our lifetime. And God is even there for us, during the times that we may reject or exclude Him from our lives.

And in fact, Jesus loves us so much that He willingly suffered 5,480 wounds as a result of His Passion and Crucifixion so that we may be able to experience eternal life in Heaven through His Resurrection, for each and every one of us, as mortals on this earth. Jesus will never give up on us, since He loves us so infinitely and unconditionally in spite of all of our faults, failings and sins.

As a teenager, I chose to follow Jesus, and to include God in my daily life. But as I grew older, due to an irrational fear of the suffering that I believed being a Disciple of Jesus would entail, I detracted from the path of righteousness for most of my life. I also succumbed to pressure from extended family members as well and as a result, I failed to live my life in accordance with the Way, the Truth and the Life.

However, as soon as Jesus had enlightened me of my plight, through the Grace of God, my path was made straight again with

His help which, in turn, allowed me to continue to follow the path of righteousness and ultimately, to be able to attain true happiness in life.

I have arrived at the strong realization that life is indeed worth living. Life is definitely, and without a doubt, a most precious commodity that should always be treasured, cherished and appreciated.

Through my vision of Jesus on the Cross in the Flesh, over a year ago now, I received one of the greatest privileges, blessings and honours of being able to experience God's love.

And after being made privy to partake in the love of Christ, I firmly believe that if all mortals in this world were to experience the love that Jesus shares with each and every one of us, our souls would reciprocate this extraordinarily intense love, without a doubt, which is far greater than the human heart can ever possibly hope to experience.

Our souls were created by God to need love. And through being loved by Jesus, this actually enables us, as mortals, to feel most secure, comforted, at peace and to be able to experience true happiness in life.

If we earnestly open our hearts to Jesus, accept God's invitation when He draws us to Him, turn to Our Lord, Jesus Christ, whenever we require His help or assistance, welcome and include God in our daily lives, and place all of our faith and trust in God, Jesus will never reject or abandon us, and He will prepare a place for us in God's Kingdom after we become deceased and pass from this life and into the next.

And I would like to take this opportunity, at this point in time, to reiterate that it's God's intention to save each and every one of our souls from the Fires of Hell. Jesus is our Shepherd, and we are His Sheep.

As mortals, we must never be afraid to become a Disciple of Jesus, as I was for so many years. And as a result of having successfully overcome all of my trials and tribulations in life to date, I have learnt that Jesus will, in fact, hold our hand throughout our life journey, and since nothing is impossible through God, Jesus can always help us, even when mankind cannot.

God existed before all else and since He created mankind, and the world in which we live, Jesus has the ability and power to resolve any problems that we may experience in life. If we acquire the fortitude to ask God for His assistance, place all of our faith, hope and trust in Jesus, and believe that anything is possible through God, then miracles can and will occur, as a result.

After encountering another dark tunnel, in desperation, I turned to St Michael the Archangel for his intercession and help. And being so spiritually close to him, I knew, without a doubt, that he would be able to help me. Consequently, I prayed fervently to this magnificent Archangel to assist me to move forwards with my life, and to finally be able to lay my past to rest. And my prayers were answered. St Michael the Archangel did not let me down, and since he is the Prince and Leader of the Nine Choirs of Angels and the closest Angel to God, I knew that his prayers were much more powerful than mine, and that St Michael the Archangel would be able to help me to successfully overcome my predicament.

But soon, my life took a sudden turn for the worse, once again, when Sam, most unexpectedly, received a phone call from our son's school, informing us that Michael had dislocated his patella during his physical education class. We were told that an ambulance had been called, and that a paramedic had managed to push his patella back into place, with the help of some pain relief medication.

After further investigation, an MRI showed that Michael had sustained some shallow impaction fractures in his patella, and that he had also experienced some bleeding, as a result.

After making an initial appointment with our daughter's past orthopaedic specialist, Sam and I were informed that Michael actually had loose ligaments in both of his kneecaps which could possibly result in the occurrence of further episodes of dislocation.

After the consultation, I became most upset. I cried in the privacy of my bedroom, whilst holding onto my favourite and most treasured Statue of my Mother Mary holding Baby Jesus in Her arms which I had received as a gift from my grandmother (my mother's mother) whilst she was still a mortal on this earth, many years ago.

And looking up, with tears streaming down my face, I suddenly and most unexpectedly experienced a vision of the Sacred Heart of Jesus. In my vision, I saw Jesus wearing a bright red garment with His Sacred Heart being exposed. Jesus then proceeded to open His Arms, inviting me to come to Him, so that our Lord and God may comfort me during my time of need.

On the actual day of my 53rd Birthday, I experienced a most unusual supernatural occurrence which had never happened before. I was at home, in my bedroom, when suddenly, I felt the strong presence of Angels around me. I could definitely sense a number of Angels surrounding me, and their presence radiated such love towards me.

And I knew exactly which of God's most Holy Angels had suddenly surrounded me on my Birthday.

I could strongly feel the presence of Prince St Michael, my own personal Guardian Angel, St Gabriel the Archangel as well as St Raphael the Healer. I felt most blessed, privileged and honoured that God had actually bestowed upon me a gift of possessing a heightened sense of awareness which actually allowed me to sense and be attuned to supernatural events and phenomena. The intense love which was being radiated from so many different Angels was such a uniquely beautiful and extraordinary experience that it caused me to become rather emotional at the time.

Over time, I became extremely 'clingy' to St Michael the Archangel, as well as to Jesus. I had arrived at the strong realization that becoming clingy to friends and constantly discussing my problems with them was not in my own best interests, nor was it in their own, because in the end, all that I really managed to do was to drive them away with my countless problems and melancholic behaviour, especially since nobody really seemed to be able to help me to resolve my seemingly unresolvable problems anyway.

And so, I learnt to always pray to St Michael the Archangel whenever I was experiencing problems or great suffering in life, including the times that I was feeling melancholy, distressed, uneasy, disheartened, disillusioned, or even broken-hearted. And St Michael the Archangel always managed to help me, never failing to answer my prayers, and he was always there for me when I needed him the most.

At the arrival of the end of term school holidays, we enjoyed watching a movie together on television each night, as a family. But whilst sitting on the couch, one evening, I suddenly felt extremely drawn to St Michael the Archangel. It was as though I was in desperate need of his comfort and protection which struck me as being a most unusual occurrence, since I had absolutely no idea as to why I was feeling this particular way at the time.

And after I went to bed that night, my emotions remained unchanged. But what baffled me the most was that I failed to understand why I had felt the need to be so protected and comforted by St Michael the Archangel. Nevertheless, I prayed to him regardless, and asked Prince St Michael to provide me with his continual comfort and protection.

However, the following day, when I awoke in the morning, I experienced feelings of extreme uneasiness in my soul. And so, I prayed to St Michael the Archangel again, for his comfort and protection, since I was still feeling particularly clingy to him.

Shortly afterwards, whilst I was sitting at my computer and my children were still fast asleep, I suddenly felt the floor move under my feet. It took me by complete surprise, and I wasn't sure if I had imagined this but then, when I felt the floor move for the second consecutive time, I began to panic since I failed to understand the direct cause of this at the time.

However, everything soon became crystal clear to me when the house began to rattle loudly, and I immediately knew that we were experiencing an earthquake. I raced over to my children to check on them, but the earthquake had already awoken them both as a result of their beds being shaken, the rattling of the blinds against their windows, and a toy had even been knocked off my son's tallboy in his bedroom from the strength of the earthquake which had lasted for a period of approximately twenty seconds in duration.

The epicentre for the earthquake was 180 km away, and although three consecutive earthquakes had actually occurred, we had only experienced the effects of the largest earthquake which was measured at 5.9 on the Richter Scale, and was the strongest earthquake on record in my state since European Settlement. It had occurred 10 km below the Earth's surface, and was also felt in neighbouring states.

However, initially, I had failed to recognize that an earthquake was actually occurring at the time, since earthquakes were rarely experienced in my state. A few buildings in the city had been damaged, and had even partially collapsed. But our house had sustained no damage as a consequence of the earthquake. And it was only afterwards, that I suddenly understood why I had become so clingy to St Michael the Archangel, although unbeknown to me at the time. I strongly believe that Prince St Michael had protected my family from harm, and had kept us safe during the occurrence of the earthquake.

Prince St Michael is an extremely powerful Angel of God. He was responsible for helping me to overcome the problems that I had encountered in my life. I now have the freedom to focus on my husband and two children whom I adore more than words can possibly express, and make my own decisions in life without having to constantly consult with my extended family members due to my newfound independence. I also have the freedom to become as religious and spiritually close to Jesus as He will allow me to be as well as to become my true self at fifty-two years of age.

'To Know God is to Love God', is a phrase that we may have heard many times during our lifetime. But what does this well-known phrase really mean in terms of the Roman Catholic Faith? Just as we, as mortals, grow to love our family members as we get to know them at a more personal level, we can also grow to know and love God, more and more, as we become spiritually closer to Him over time if we always turn to God in our hour of need, include Him in our everyday lives, and love God with all of our heart, with all of our soul, with all of our mind and with all of our strength.

# CHAPTER 24

But what does it really mean to love God with all of our heart, with all of our soul, with all of our mind and with all of our strength?

Does it mean that we, as mortals, should always place God, first and foremost, in our lives and even before our own families, relatives, friends, foe, careers, jobs, position and status in life, financial woes, hobbies, interests and leisure activities? And the answer to this question, in black and white terms is: "Yes, definitely and without a doubt."

If we truly love God with all of our heart, soul, mind and strength, then we shall be rewarded, by God, both on Earth as well as in Heaven, where we will take our place at God's Table which Jesus has prepared for us to share in His Banquet.

This morning, during my usual daily prayer session, I experienced yet another two-part vision. Again, I was made privy to witness the Gateway to Heaven where I saw the most realistic looking white fluffy clouds gradually moving across the sky. But this time, during my vision, I was not shocked and I felt a most intense sense of serenity, peace, tranquillity, comfort and happiness overpower me.

However, whilst experiencing the second part of my vision in succession, I witnessed Hell, and there are no words in the English language that can possibly ever hope to describe its repugnance to me. I was totally shocked and horrified at seeing a large black cauldron containing a mixture of red and black molten lava, in which a soul was trapped inside. Although I could only see the mere shadow of this particular soul, I was also made privy to be able to see the shadow of Satan Himself who was standing beside the cauldron, stirring the molten lava with an object strongly resembling that of a long stick.

But in relation to the mortals who love God with all of their heart, with all of their mind, with all of their soul and with all of their strength, and who genuinely always try their utmost to obey God's Commandments to the very best of their abilities, their souls will be given the greatest privilege and honour of being able to encounter God Face-to-Face in Heaven, where they will experience His love, first and foremost, peace, comfort, happiness and joy for all eternity.

However, before I continue, I would just like to emphasize that most souls must spend time in Purgatory first, in order to be purified, before being deemed worthy, by God, of entering through the Gateway to Heaven.

These souls must undergo a purification process which involves extreme pain, suffering and remorse for the sins that were committed on Earth as mortals. Sins are highlighted in Purgatory, and as soon as souls become purified, they progress to Heaven where they will finally be able to experience God's unbearably intense love, peace, tranquillity, comfort, joy and happiness, for which only God can provide.

Sadly, for those mortals who choose not to follow the path of righteousness and the Way, the Truth and the Life, such souls suffer the most intense, excruciating and unbearable form of relentless and constant torture, torment, ridicule and pain, administered by Satan Himself in Hell, that is so intolerable that these souls actually beg God to allow them to die, since the pain is too great to be able to be endured. But their torture must be sustained infinitively since souls can never die, and live for all eternity.

And I strongly believe that many mortals are completely unaware of the fact that once these souls have been dispatched to Hell after having faced God on Judgement Day in reparation for the grave and deadly sins that they have committed whilst mortals on this earth which have offended God at the highest level, the time they spend in Hell is for all eternity. These souls are never given the opportunity to be able to progress to Heaven, as souls in Purgatory are able to do. Their final destination, being Hell, is a one-way street which leads to a dead end, encompassing no way of return.

Saints, on the other hand, are so pure in body, mind, spirit and soul, that they actually bypass Purgatory, immediately entering through the Gateway to Heaven, since there is no need for Saints to spend any time in Purgatory to purify their souls.

Another religious dream which I would like to bring to your attention, that I experienced most recently, encompassed two alligators and interestingly enough, this is actually the second time that I have dreamt about alligators/crocodiles during my lifetime.

I distinctly remember being upstairs in the office area of a hospital building discussing my relative to a lady whom I failed to recognize. She was sitting behind a desk, and I was attempting to justify, to this particular lady, the reasons as to why I had chosen not to receive the coronavirus vaccines, and she was frowning at me in response. However, in the end, the lady accepted my rationale, and I went downstairs into the hospital foyer area.

Suddenly, I saw the wooden double doors swing open, and a very large alligator came crawling into the hospital foyer at a really fast pace. I just stared at the alligator in amazement, and although I did experience an element of fear, I was not actually terrified at this point in time.

All of the surrounding people were screaming and running in different directions in an attempt to avoid the alligator. But then, shortly afterwards, another alligator of similar appearance, came crawling into the foyer area and consequently, I became extremely frightened and ran outside the building for my own personal safety. Walking along the footpath, I headed up the street, and contemplated catching a tram home. And after checking my purse, I realized that I had more than enough money in order to be able to buy a tram ticket home. And it was at this point that I suddenly awoke from my dream.

Shortly after experiencing this religious dream, I arrived at the strong realization that the two alligators which had crawled into the hospital building were a representation of two of my close relatives.

And two days after the occurrence of my dream, a relative rang Sam's mobile and tried to force me to get the coronavirus vaccine, through my husband, which failed to surprise me, since it was in my relative's nature to try her utmost to coerce me to do things that were against my will.

And it was soon apparent to me that my recent dream which had occurred only two days prior, was already beginning to come true. Sam was forced to justify to my close relative the reasons as to why I was so opposed to getting vaccinated.

However, on this same day, another close relative called me afterwards and recorded a long voicemail message which she left on my mobile, regarding becoming vaccinated. My relative tried her utmost to convince me to join her, my other close relative and her partner to get vaccinated on the same day that they were booked to receive one of the available vaccines. In her message, my relative also mentioned that I could die if I were to contract the coronavirus, and that my children would be left to grow up without a mother or alternatively, I could end up on a ventilator, as a result.

Before long, I realized that my dream was actually a prophecy since initially, my close relative had tried to force me to become vaccinated against my will, (the first alligator that entered the hospital foyer) and then my other relative (who was the second alligator) had followed suit, soon after.

Most unexpectedly, I experienced yet another religious dream which was of a completely different nature to my previous spiritual dream.

I remember walking amidst a large crowd of people with my mother in a shopping centre. Suddenly, a lady aggressively pushed in front of my mother, bumping into her in the process. My mother rebuked the lady for displaying such inappropriate behaviour and in response, the lady turned around and slapped my mother in the face. Hence, I became extremely upset, as a result. And consequently, I searched for a security guard in order to be able to report this lady for physically assaulting my mother, but I couldn't seem to find one anywhere.

Finally, I noticed a female security guard walking down a nearby staircase to whom I quickly explained the series of events which had taken place. And shaking her head in response, the security guard said that the lady would only refuse to disclose her name, if asked, and that there was nothing that she could really do to help us. And sure enough, whilst the security guard was reprimanding this lady for her abusive behaviour towards my mother, she simply remained silent when asked to give her name. As a result, I gave up and left with my mother.

It was no wonder that I felt as though the only choice that I could have made at the time of my forced hospital admission, over a year ago, was to turn to God to the extreme, in order to escape from the current world in which I lived on Earth and enter into God's Supernatural World which contained only love, peace, tranquillity, comfort, joy and happiness.

However, despite all of the tremendous suffering that I have constantly and relentlessly been forced to endure during my lifetime, I have realized that my autobiography does, in fact, contain a happy ending. And I had consciously made the decision not to publish my book until I had achieved true happiness in life since I have always found happy endings to be most encouraging and inspirational myself.

Most unexpectedly, whilst in the process of editing the manuscript for this book, I suddenly felt such an intense and overwhelming love for St Michael the Archangel. I became extremely emotional at the time, so much so, that tears began streaming down my face as a result of experiencing so much love for this truly magnificent Archangel who was continually helping to heal the emotional wounds that my extended family members had inflicted upon me over the years. And this led me to arrive at the strong realization that my soul was actually responding to the intense love that St Michael the Archangel was radiating to me at the time.

So, in conclusion then, I have arrived at the strong realization that my life actually does contain a happy ending, although not the ending that I had expected to experience.

And I have realized that it is of the utmost importance to me, since undergoing my strong conversion, to focus all of my attention on serving God, accomplishing God's Will, which includes writing this book in the hope that it will be able to inspire others who are on a similar life journey to mine, as well as to spend as much time as possible with my wonderful husband and children, whom I will always cherish and treasure for the rest of my life.

I have been so blessed in being able to encounter God through my countless visions, religious dreams and spiritual experiences.

I am also of the belief that it's vital to be grateful to God for all of the precious and invaluable gifts that He has bestowed upon us whilst mortals on this earth, and to learn to appreciate and focus our attention on everything that we have already received in life, rather than on what we perceive that we still need or want, and have not yet attained in our lives.

And this reminds me of the time that I had so desperately wished to become a mother, but initially failed to become pregnant.

However, through Our Lady's intercession, and the miracle of the Holy Water from Lourdes, I was blessed to become the mother of a most beautiful and precious baby girl. And as a result of feeling so much gratitude towards God for answering my prayers, I had not dared to ask Him for another child. But through God's great mercy, compassion and love, Jesus bestowed upon me the gift of being able to conceive another child - a son who is also most pure in heart and soul, through the Grace of God.

I truly love Jesus for so many different reasons, but especially because we, as mortals, have to fight to become spiritually close to God which verifies the magnitude of the freewill that God has bestowed upon each and every one of us from birth. God invites all of us, as Children of God, to be able to experience a close spiritual relationship with Him, and we have been given the freedom to either accept or decline His invitation.

God will never force us to believe in Him, love Him, include Him in our daily lives or even turn to Him during our time of need. But throughout our lives, Jesus will grant us multiple chances to repent, to come to Him, and to develop a close spiritual relationship with Him.

After having experienced a form of ecstasy recently, during the night, I have arrived at the strong realization that when I had turned to God to the extreme, over a year ago, and displayed most unusual behaviour, I was actually going in and out of ecstasy continually, and sometimes I had even remained in ecstasy for an extended period of time.

And during my forced hospital stay, I had spent most of each and every day in ecstasy which had assisted me to be able to cope with being in such a horrifically frightening and terrifying environment, and it also brought me so much closer to St Michael the Archangel whom I knew, was always with me to protect and help me. And consequently, I became even more spiritually close to God, as a result.

But it wasn't long before I underwent another difficult trial whereby, I suddenly became extremely upset regarding my son's kneecap dislocation which I have already mentioned in more detail, earlier in this book. I remember being most melancholy at the time, since I had felt such a vast amount of compassion for my son, especially since dislocations are said to be so physically painful when they occur. And it was breaking my heart that Michael had had to experience such a traumatic event in his early teenage years. Hence, going upstairs to pray to Jesus in the privacy of my bedroom, I turned to Him in desperation, and begged Jesus for His help. I begged Him to heal my son's patella so that Michael would never experience any further episodes of kneecap dislocations in the future.

Whilst praying with my eyes open, I suddenly experienced another vision which encompassed the Sacred Heart of Jesus. In my vision, Jesus was wearing a bright red garment, and His Sacred Heart was exposed. But then immediately afterwards, I experienced yet another vision in which I saw Jesus wearing a pure white garment, only in this vision, brightly coloured light was being emanated from the Sacred Heart of Jesus. Experiencing these two visions in succession were, in fact, messages from God informing me that Jesus was comforting me through my time of trial and great suffering.

However, in becoming spiritually close to Jesus, and as a result of having reached a Mystical Union with Christ, these immeasurable personal achievements, on my part, have actually allowed me to finally experience true happiness in life.

Since becoming spiritually close to Jesus, and through my heightened sense of awareness in being able to discern the presence of all three of God's magnificent Archangels – Prince St Michael, St Raphael the Healer and St Gabriel Archangel, including that of my own personal Guardian Angel, who constantly surround and protect me, I know, without a doubt, that Jesus will continually assist me to sail my vessel smoothly through the troubled waters of life, and its most stormy seas. Jesus will not only calm the magnitudinous waves that constantly rock and threaten to capsize my boat, but He will also prevent me from being thrown into the sea, to sink below the water surface and drown, as a consequence.

Our Lord and God will continually hold our hand during our time of great suffering; Jesus will never abandon us when we need Him the most; He will not only lighten our burden, but Jesus will also assist us to travel along the path of righteousness, in accordance with the Way, the Truth and the Life since Jesus Christ is, without a doubt, the Light of our World, and He will help us to reach our final destination, being Heaven, where we shall experience His intense love, peace, comfort, joy and happiness, infinitively and for all eternity.

Jesus did not endure His Passion and Crucifixion for only a small number of mortals who exist on this earth. But rather, He died on the Cross for every single one of us, since it's God's intention to save each soul from the Fires of Hell, so that we may all experience eternal life through Jesus.

By possessing a holy fear of God, and of His most powerful Archangels, we are acknowledging their true existence, magnificence and power, as well as our belief in supernatural occurrences.

It would be most unrealistic to expect life to contain no suffering since Jesus, Who is God Himself, suffered 5,480 wounds in His Passion and Crucifixion, reopening Heaven, as a result.

I have also arrived at the powerful realization that, in the past, I had constantly held the most unrealistic expectations towards others in my life, particularly and especially during my times of great need when, in fact, only Jesus was truly capable of assisting me to successfully resolve all of my problems.

And as a result of having experienced the two consecutive visions encompassing the Sacred Heart of Jesus, I have realized that only Jesus could really help me by completely alleviating my pain and suffering.

Through fervent prayer, Jesus, Prince St Michael, St Raphael the Healer and St Gabriel Archangel were all responsible for traversing my immeasurable and most unbearable pain and suffering, and helped me to overcome all of my trials and tribulations in life.

So, in essence, only Jesus has the true power to 'resurrect us from the dead', through His constant help and the intercession of His most Holy Angels, in our time of need.

But it wasn't long before I experienced another difficult period in my life which caused me to feel most overwhelmed, and I was in desperate need of finding the Light since darkness was beginning to prevail, once more. But after attending the evening Mass at our local parish, with my family, Jesus actually enlightened me in Church through the Readings, the Second Reading in particular.

# CHAPTER 25

But an extract from the Second Reading, as outlined below, gave me the foresight that I so desperately needed in order to be able to move forwards with my life:

Ephesians 4:17,20-24

"That, however, is not the way of life you learned 21 when you heard about Christ and were taught in him in accordance with the truth that is in Jesus. 22 You were taught, with regard to your former way of life, to put off your old self, which is being corrupted by its deceitful desires; 23 to be made new in the attitude of your minds; 24 and to put on the new self, created to be like God in true righteousness and holiness."

Therefore, I realized that what I really needed to do, at this point in time, was to let go of my old self in order to be able to become my new self. And by letting go of my old self, I was also simultaneously laying my past to rest, enabling me to be able to focus all of my attention on the present and future instead.

Hence, I must become my new self in order to be able to successfully accomplish the missions that God has assigned me in life.

I soon arrived at the extremely strong conclusion that I would simply be most unable to accomplish this on my own, however, no matter how hard I tried, or wanted to change my current thought processes.

Therefore, in desperation, I prayed daily, and sometimes even multiple times, to St Michael the Archangel to assist me as I know that his prayers are extremely powerful. Since Prince St Michael is a Messenger of God, the closest Angel to God, and the most courageous out of the billions of Angels that God created in His Army of Heavenly Hosts, I immediately knew that, through his constant intercession, St Michael the Archangel could alleviate my continual and irrational fears, especially since nothing is impossible through God, and Prince St Michael is the Angel of Peace as well as of Courage.

And so, over time, I learnt to place all of my faith and trust in St Michael the Archangel because in doing so, I was simultaneously placing all of my faith and trust in God, the Creator of our world and of all that is good, pure and holy.

And after a period of time had passed, I noticed that my thought processes were slowly beginning to change for the better.

In the past, my irrational fears had caused a most negative impact on my thought processes, and a fear of life itself was a true obstacle which I somehow needed to be able to overcome. In fact, my irrational fears were blocking my ability to be able to experience genuine happiness and peace in my soul, but as a result of my prayers to St Michael the Archangel, and his constant intercession, he assisted me to allay each one of my fears gradually over time.

Prince St Michael provided me with the necessary fortitude that I needed to acquire in order to take up my Cross and follow Jesus, and to be able to bear all of my suffering. And in doing so, I know that I shall be able to experience true happiness in life, both on Earth and in Heaven for all eternity.

And as a direct result of the supernatural occurrences that encompass my life in the form of multiple and countless visions, religious dreams and spiritual experiences, it can be said that I am actually experiencing Heaven on Earth, as a result, and I shall always consider myself to be the most blessed and privileged mortal in existence on this earth and in society today.

Overall, God fulfilled my insatiable desire and need to be loved unconditionally; Jesus was always there for me when I needed Him the most, just as He has continually been there for me throughout my entire lifetime, and even during the times when I had believed that I was totally alone in my suffering. Jesus has never abandoned, rejected or belittled me to raise His own status, nor has He ever caused me to feel as though I was an unimportant, insignificant and worthless human being, as well as a waste of space on this earth.

But instead, Jesus had the opposite effect on me since God exalts the humble, and He allowed me to experience His countless and multiple visions, religious dreams and spiritual experiences which I will always treasure, cherish and value immeasurably, and more than anything else in this entire world.

In addition, I would like to take this opportunity to emphasize and reiterate that I am writing this book not only to inspire others who are on a similar life journey to mine, but also to be of assistance to those who have been struggling perhaps with their faith in God, for those mortals who have turned away from God and blame Him specifically for their misfortune and unfortunate circumstances, as well as for those who are desperately searching to find the true meaning of life.

Beauty is in the eye of the beholder. My sibling had found the fake clouds in my personal Apparition encompassing the Mother of God, 'beautiful'. Personally, however, I found the clouds to look most unrealistic and fake since I am intoxicated with God's love instead. The superficial attractions instigated by Satan are extremely unattractive to me, more repulsive than I can ever hope to express in words.

I believe that mortals have become so concerned with focussing on their own selfish needs and wants that they have forgotten what the true meaning of life is actually about – to build on the Grace that Jesus has so generously bestowed upon each and every one of us through Baptism so that He can prepare a place for us in Heaven.

I am but a grain of salt in the Earth's Crust; a grain of sand in the vast and infinite sand dunes that encompass the Earth; a mere drop of water in the infinite spray of the oceans. I am but a tiny voice amidst a choir of voices – only one voice amidst billions of voices that make up the core of society on Earth, but a voice that wishes to be heard since my voice can lead to the salvation of souls.

I would like to emphasize that Satan and his billions of demons roam this earth in a constant and relentless attempt to derail mortals from following the path of righteousness so that Satan may taunt, torture and inflict unspeakable pain and suffering in Hell on the mortals who have chosen to follow the path which leads to destruction and encompasses the darkness of sin.

Recently, I arrived at a revelation that God never actually allows us to go over and beyond our threshold for tolerance for the pain and suffering that we may endure during our lifetime as mortals on this earth. And as testament to this, I would like to use an analogy incorporating childbirth, and the actual process of labour, to reinforce my level of thinking.

In relation to the process of childbirth for my first natural birth, I strongly believed that the pain would be too great for me to be able to bear continuously, and over an extended period of time. Therefore, I opted to have an epidural during the early labour stages, after experiencing the first few pangs of labour pains.

And so, for the duration of my six-and-a-half hour labour, I was mainly pain-free and I never thought twice about making this decision for my own well-being, until I experienced my second natural birth, more than three years down the track.

But it's most noteworthy here to mention that I faced a completely different scenario during my second natural birth. And this was at a time when my obstetrician had led me to believe that my entire labour would only last around two-three hours in duration. Consequently, he actually advised me not to opt for an epidural since he was confident that my labour would be relatively short, and that it would be almost too late to ask for an epidural once labour had already begun to take its course.

And surprisingly, after undergoing an induced labour, initially I found that I could actually tolerate the labour pains since they were so intermittent and far apart. And consequently, I was rather confident that I would be able to handle the labour pains throughout the entire process quite easily, without the aid of an epidural.

But as my labour progressed, and the labour pains increased in intensity and became more frequent, I began to wonder if I had made the right decision in not opting to have an epidural at the beginning of my labour. I started to become more and more exhausted, and I soon realized that I was not going to experience the short labour that my obstetrician had initially anticipated.

And after a period of approximately five-and-a-half hours had lapsed, my labour pains had become so intense and frequent that I felt as though I simply couldn't bear the pain any longer. I strongly believed that I had reached my threshold for tolerance for pain and suffering. And the moment that I had told the midwife that I just couldn't do this anymore since I was finding the pain most unbearable to tolerate, she immediately informed me that she had been waiting for me to reach this conclusion and stage of labour, since it basically meant that the baby was deemed ready to be delivered into the world.

Therefore, the labour pains experienced by mothers in childbirth is a prime example and verification that once our suffering reaches an unbearable/intolerable level in life, Jesus alleviates our pain and suffering and is always there for us when we need Him the most.

# CHAPTER 26

Presently and currently, I received another health scare which I would like to take this opportunity to explain in some detail – a scare which actually turned my entire world upside down.

After having my yearly check-up for my countless moles scattered throughout my body, the dermatologist found one mole on my neck which he recommended that I remove as a precaution so that we didn't have to watch it anymore. But I had basically received the all clear.

Soon afterwards, whilst in the bathroom, I noticed an odd-looking reddish-brown mole underneath my right upper arm which looked rather suspicious even to an untrained eye. I showed the mole to my local general practitioner who said that the mole was benign but due to its composition, there was a 5% chance that this mole could become a melanoma at some time in the future. I asked him if it would be a good idea to also have this mole removed along with the other mole on my neck simultaneously and he immediately agreed that this would be the best option.

I sent in a photo of the mole to my dermatologist to ask if it should be removed sooner than the two months that my surgery had been booked to take place. The dermatologist replied that the mole did not look suspicious and that it was okay to wait the two months to also have this mole removed.

After having the two moles removed, I received three stitches as a result of each mole removal. But upon my return to the dermatologist after a period of two weeks had lapsed, I received the biggest shock of my life when the pathology results regarding the two moles had returned. The mole on my neck was benign but the mole on my arm was in fact an early-stage melanoma in situ of superficial spreading. The entire mole had been successfully removed but I was in shock since I never expected to have a melanoma in the first place and secondly, this particular mole had only been removed as a result of my insistence.

In my view, Divine Intervention had saved me. If I had not requested that this mole be removed and if I had not found it myself, I could have died from this melanoma which could have already spread throughout my body before being discovered.

Although, I considered myself blessed to have discovered this melanoma so early, I was still terrified at having had a melanoma and I couldn't understand why God had permitted such a traumatic event and medical illness to have occurred in my life.

Initially, I was so upset at having had the melanoma that I actually considered turning away from God, as a result. But I soon realized that I was so blessed that God had saved me through the early detection of my melanoma that I just couldn't turn away from God and abandon Him.

But why has my life continued to contain so much endless and relentless suffering? And this is a question that I have asked myself over and over again for a number of years now. And I still don't really have a logical explanation in answer to this question other than since Jesus suffered 5,480 wounds during his Passion and Crucifixion, so too must we each suffer during our time on Earth which will lessen the time that we spend in Purgatory so that we may reach Heaven as our final destination, sooner rather than later.

The day after my melanoma diagnosis, I was still in shock and I couldn't believe that the mole in my right arm had been a melanoma. And in about four weeks' time, I will need to consult a surgeon to make a wider excision of healthy tissue to ensure that the melanoma has been completely removed and fails to return.

In due course, I underwent the wide excision under general anaesthetic and so I failed to experience any pain, as a result. Approximately, 1 cm was excised from the original scar to prevent the melanoma from growing back.

Two days after the surgery had been performed, I received the all clear, however, in terms of the pathology results for the wide excision and I was most thankful to God that the melanoma had not spread into the surrounding tissues.

It was a most terrifying time for me and again, I found myself being afraid to experience true happiness in life since one bad event was occurring after another consistently and relentlessly.

My biggest fear in life had actually become realized – the fear of getting cancer. And to say that I was terrified of cancer would be an understatement.

However, I soon realized that I needed to focus on the positives rather than the negatives in my life. The melanoma at least was discovered very early and my situation could have been a lot worse if the melanoma was discovered at a later date. I was beginning to realize that nothing in this world can occur unless it's God's Ordained Will or His Permitting Will and that my life was totally in God's Hands. I also arrived at the strong realization that I needed to surrender my life to Jesus and that I had no control over my own life. God, in fact, controls everything and we are nothing without God.

Overall, however, one of my main aims and goals in writing this book is to basically encourage mortals to turn to God during their hour of need, as I always have in my life, with the knowledge that God will always help us, and Jesus will never abandon us. Whenever we knock on His door, the door shall be opened to us; whenever we seek God, we shall always find Him; whenever we sincerely ask God for His infinite mercy, He shall always grant us His forgiveness.

But it's of crucial and the utmost importance to both acknowledge and understand that to 'Know Jesus is to Love Him'. And in loving God above all things, this shall continually bring us spiritually closer to God, lead to an elimination of all of our fears associated with the future and hence, enable us to be able to experience true happiness in life.

By making time, in our most busy lives, to get to know our Lord and God at a higher spiritual level, we shall essentially learn to love Jesus with all of our heart, with all of our soul, with all of our mind, with all of our strength, and with every living cell in our body, which will inevitably enrich our lives to the maximum. This will also allow our souls to be able to experience true happiness in life, as well as the peace, tranquillity, comfort, joy and above all, God's unconditional love that He created our souls to need to experience on a daily basis.

Personally, however, I know that Jesus will always guide, protect and help me to acquire the necessary courage required in order to follow Him, through the intercession of Prince St Michael. Jesus and Prince St Michael will also assist me to finally be able to let go of my past, leave my old self behind, focus on the present and future, and by virtue of my new self, strive to continually accomplish God's Will to the very best of my abilities for the remainder of my life on this earth.

In a nutshell, however, it has taken me 53 years to find my true self. I am also now becoming the person that I had always so desperately felt the need to aspire to become. I truly loathed and was ashamed of my old self.

But after having successfully overcome all of the countless trials, tribulations and great obstacles in my life, some of which had initially seemed to be insurmountable, at first, I am now convinced, without a semblance of doubt, that Jesus has always held my hand throughout my life, without realizing this to be the case in the past. Jesus was always there for me when I needed him the most; He never abandoned, rejected, belittled or controlled me in any way, shape or form. Jesus never forced me to serve Him or to devote the rest of my life in serving Him and in doing His Will; He never loved me only conditionally provided that I served and obeyed Him but instead, Jesus has always loved me unconditionally and I know, in my heart and soul, that He will always love me most unconditionally and infinitely until the day I die, as well as in the afterlife.

It's difficult for me to be able to decipher what I love the most about Jesus, since there is a myriad of reasons as to why I love God so intensely, and above all things in my life. But I believe that the answer lies in my heart and soul, much more than in my own subconscious, since my heart and soul crave, more desperately than words in the English Language are capable of describing, to be loved unconditionally, for the person that I am, for my new self, and for the person that I aspire to be in the near future.

And before jumping to conclusions in blaming God for our misfortunes and/or perhaps even considering turning away from Him, it's always a good idea to pray to Our Lord and God for His help, during these most difficult times in our lives, and ask Jesus to enlighten us if we may feel trapped by our circumstances, just as a fly/insect that becomes caught in a spider web is rarely able to escape its fate from thereon.

I also believe, deep in my heart and soul, that it's of crucial importance for every mortal on this earth to try their utmost to place all of their faith and trust in God, and to remember that it's always God's intention to save each and every one of our souls from the Fires of Hell so that we may experience His infinite and unconditional love, peace, comfort, tranquillity, joy and happiness in the purest form, for all eternity in Heaven.

It's so easy for us, as mortals, to misjudge our Lord and God, and to blame Him for everything bad/negative that may occur in our everyday lives, especially if we can only see the smaller picture at the time, rather than the bigger picture.

Instead, I strongly urge all of my readers who may find themselves in a dire situation or circumstance in life, to think twice before possibly becoming angry, disgruntled or disillusioned with God, wanting to turn away and/or blame Him for our misery, melancholy and extreme unhappiness.

Our misery may solely, in fact, be purely and simply, as a result of Satan trying his utmost to take a stronghold of our lives in an attempt to mislead, deceive and detract us from the path of righteousness, so as to drag us down to Hell in the afterlife where Satan can ridicule, taunt and torture these souls far beyond their tolerance levels for pain and suffering, and not just for a finite period of time, however, but for all eternity, with no periods of reprieve or relief, since souls can never die nor can they ever be destroyed in any way, shape or form.

Therefore, it's of the utmost importance that we make the effort to seek God, knock on His door, earnestly ask Jesus for the forgiveness of our sins and for His continual assistance in our lives since Jesus will never reject or turn us away when we come to Him, unlike mortals who possess the ability to do this, over and over again, as I have experienced countless times in the past.

And I urge all of you, as Children of God, to please remember that Jesus can always help us in any given circumstance/situation, even when mankind cannot. God will help us to overcome each and every single one of our trials and tribulations in life, no matter how great or small they may be, and show us the compassion, love, understanding and gentleness that only Jesus is truly capable of expressing. And above all, Jesus will provide us with the comfort and reassurance that our souls crave to experience the most, during these extremely difficult times in our lives.

But with God's Grace and continual help, I have finally become the person that I was always destined to be in life. I am proud of the person that I am now, and I will always aspire to be the best person that I can possibly be and the person that God has permitted me to become through His infinite mercy.

It has also been revealed to me that by undergoing great suffering in life on Earth, and by enduring our many trials and tribulations, our souls are actually becoming more purified in the process and as a result, after we become deceased, this has the cause and effect of shortening our time in Purgatory overall. Hence, our souls will undergo so much less suffering in Purgatory, and will progress to Heaven much sooner, as a direct consequence of this.

By reflecting on my past, and through focussing on the tremendous and, at times, unbearable suffering that I have constantly had to endure throughout my lifetime, I can confidently say that I am now able to see everything in a different light to when I first began writing the story of my life. All of my great and intolerable suffering has been worthwhile, just to have been given the greatest honour, privilege and blessing of being able to experience God's love through my countless visions, religious dreams and spiritual experiences.

Therefore, in essence, my dream encompassing my personal Apparition with the Immaculate Virgin Mary, the Mother of God, has in nearly all aspects, finally become reality. Admittedly, however, it took a long period of time, about fifteen months in duration, for the prophecy to slowly unfold almost in its entirety. But I would like to strongly emphasize that my pain and suffering over the past fifteen months has been appeased and alleviated by

Jesus, Prince St Michael and my Mother Mary Herself.

There was a point in time in which I was beginning to doubt whether or not I would ever be able to experience the segment in my dream whereby Our Lady was transformed into becoming young again. However, I am now optimistically waiting to experience this part of my dream in the future.

It's of crucial importance to realize, acknowledge and understand that only Jesus is truly capable of assisting us in any given life circumstance/situation, and that nothing is impossible through God. If we constantly pray to the three Archangels, Prince St Michael, St Raphael the Healer and St Gabriel Archangel, as I do, on a daily basis, then these magnificent Archangels will also answer our prayers and will simultaneously assist us to become spiritually closer to Jesus, as a result.

In essence, Jesus continues to assist me in my daily life. I am nothing without God and through the intercession of Prince St Michael, St Gabriel Archangel and St Raphael the Healer (who are my life support) these magnificent Archangels are truly capable of helping to resolve the constant and relentless problems that continually occur in my life.

Overall, however, Jesus Christ was the inspiration for this book and it was He Who inspired me, through accomplishing His Will, to tell my story to the world, which is based completely and utterly on fact rather than fiction.

I shall always live in the hope that this spiritual book will be able to inspire others who are on a similar life journey to mine, and that it will encourage as many mortals on this earth as possible, to reach out to Jesus during their hour of need, since God will always help those who seek His assistance; Jesus will never abandon us, and God will always open the door to those mortals who, of their own freewill, choose to knock on His door.

Upon reflection, it causes me great melancholy to ponder the current state of the world in which we live and in particular, those mortals who either don't believe in God, have permanently rejected or turned away from God or refuse to acknowledge God's existence due to being disillusioned with God. But our souls were created to need love, and when our love is not reciprocated by mortals, then the void/empty space that has been left in our hearts can only be truly filled by our Lord and God, and His most Holy Angels.

We must never be afraid to love Jesus, to follow Him and to allow God to fill the empty space in our hearts that mortals leave behind when they reject us since God will always love us unconditionally and infinitely.

Jesus will always rejoice at the return of lost sheep to His Flock, many of whom have been scattered far and wide, as Jesus is our Shepherd and His intention is to save each and every single one of us, as mortals on this earth. Jesus is infinitely merciful and He will never give up on us, even during the times that we may have given up on Him.

Recently, I experienced a number of visions relating to the true physical appearances of the four Archangels who are largely undocumented in the Teachings of the Roman Catholic Church and who stand before the Throne of God.

In relation to my vision encompassing Archangel 1, he is actually part animal and part human. He has the upper body of a lion including the head of a lion, the upper paws of a lion but he retains the body of a man from the waist downwards which is more humanlike. However, Archangel 1 also has a lion's tail attached to his lower body.

Archangel 2 is also part animal and part human. He has the upper body of a tiger including the head of a tiger, the upper paws of a tiger but he retains the body of a man from the waist downwards, which is more humanlike. However, Archangel 2 also has a tiger's tail attached to his lower body.

Whilst eating my dinner, I suddenly experienced a vision of Archangel 3 - one of the Seven Archangels who stand before the Throne of God. This magnificent Archangel is part bird and part human. He has the head of an eagle, including yellow eyes, a large hooked beak, pure white feathery wings as his hands, but he retains the body of a man from the waist downwards and he wears close-fitting white leggings on his legs, except he has golden talons on his bird-like feet. However, Archangel 3 also has a wedge-tailed eagle's tail attached to his lower body.

One morning, I experienced another vision, and my vision encompassed the true physical appearance of Archangel 4 who is also part animal and part human. He has the upper body of an elephant including the head of an elephant, his front legs are elephant-like but he retains the body of a man from the waist downwards which is more humanlike. However, Archangel 4 also has an elephant's tail attached to his lower body.

Archangel 5 is St Raphael the Healer whilst Archangel 6 is St Gabriel Archangel.

Archangel 7 is actually Prince St Michael who is the Prince and Leader of the Nine Choirs of Angels, and the most powerful out of all of the billions of Angels encompassing God's most Holy Army of Heavenly Hosts.

## CHAPTER 27

You may be wondering as to why I love Jesus, Who is God Himself, above all things in my life, and why I had wished to die instantaneously just to be with Him upon experiencing the vision of Jesus on the Cross in the Flesh, over a year ago now?

Well, it's extremely difficult for me to be able to pinpoint one reason in particular, in answer to my question above and therefore, I must discuss my response in more detail in relation to why I have chosen to take up my Cross and follow Jesus for the remainder of my life on this earth.

For starters, I was most taken aback by the immeasurable and unbearable intensity of being completely and utterly immersed in God's love through my vision. My extraordinarily intense love for Jesus, whilst encountering this vision, both overpowered and overwhelmed me beyond words, and was totally out of my control.

Therefore, first and foremost, my intense and extreme love for my Lord and God was intensified through experiencing my vision encompassing Jesus on the Cross in the Flesh.

Furthermore, His gentle, compassionate, forgiving, merciful and loving nature has drawn me to Him, so much so, that again my spiritual attachment to Jesus is totally and completely beyond my control and can be likened to bees to honey.

His Passion and Crucifixion are both testament and verification for His selflessness when Jesus suffered 5,480 wounds for each and every one of us, as mortals on this earth, out of His own freewill, in order to reopen Heaven and make atonement for the sins of Adam and Eve, and for all of mankind.

And yet, there are still mortals in existence who reject Jesus, and don't obey His Commandments. And I ask each and every one of you, as my readers, this most important question: "Is it really too much to ask for each of us, as mortals, to observe the two most important Commandments that Jesus mentions in Biblical times: To love God with all of your heart, with all of your soul and with all of your mind, and to love your neighbour as yourself?" Personally, I think not.

Jesus provided us with the ultimate sacrifice – His Life – so that we can share in eternal life with Him and experience God's peace, tranquillity, comfort, joy, true happiness and above all, His unconditional and infinite love for all eternity.

Furthermore, "Do material possessions, great wealth, power, position and status in life, greed, vanity and pride, truly and genuinely enrich our lives, and grant us the peace, tranquillity, joy, happiness, comfort and love that our souls undeniably need to experience on a daily basis?" Again, personally, I think not since I would much rather encounter another vision or spiritual experience encompassing God's love at the highest level and intensity instead, especially since being loved by Jesus gives me true happiness in life.

And I would also much prefer Jesus to prepare a place for me at His Banquet in Paradise after I become deceased than for me to actually possess great wealth or status on Earth because in this way, I shall be able to continue to experience God's unconditional love, constantly and forever.

It's crucial to remember that life on Earth is only finite but the afterlife, and life in Heaven, is infinite. And after we become deceased, we cannot bring any of the material possessions that we have accumulated on Earth with us to Heaven. Therefore, by taking this into consideration, I would like to ask my readers this question to ponder: "Why do we need to acquire such wealth and material possessions in the first place, when life on Earth is only finite?"

But it's important to make the distinction that God can also provide us with everything that we need on Earth, as well as in Heaven, especially if we choose, by our own freewill, to follow the path of righteousness. And if we have our hearts set on going to Heaven in the afterlife and in living our lives according to the Way, the Truth and the Life, then we shall be rewarded by God for our labours on Earth in more ways than we can possibly ever imagine or comprehend.

In conclusion then, after 53 years of my life has already passed, I have finally discovered that there actually is Light at the end of the dark tunnel in which I have been trapped inside, and for which I had always thought that I would never be able to experience the sun shining through the clouds.

Everything is possible through God, and it was His Light that guided me through the darkness until I was able to fully emerge into the Light and bask in the warmth of the brilliant sunshine that was now surrounding me on all fronts, and encircled my life.

Jesus truly is the Light of our world and a beacon which shines brightly through the darkness of sin, human anguish, despair, fear, anxiety, melancholy and every single negative emotion that stems from Satan, and never from our Lord and God.

And I would like to reiterate at this point in time that Jesus will always be there for us when we call upon His Name; He will never abandon us during our time of need, and Jesus will always love each and every single one of us unconditionally, and more than the human heart is ever capable of being able to experience.

I have discovered the Way, the Truth and the Life, through Jesus Christ, our Lord and God, the true Saviour of our world, in becoming a Disciple of Christ.

But most importantly, in my heart and soul, I know that I am now able to finally experience the true happiness in life that I have so desperately craved to be able to experience for my 53 years of existence on this earth, through the infinite mercy and Grace of God.

And all we really need to remember, in our most busy but finite lives as mortals, is that God breathes life into every single living cell that exists on this earth since our world cannot function and/or even subsist without God's existence, and the assistance of His most Holy Angels, namely the Nine Choirs of Angels comprising of billions of Angels that encompass God's Army of Heavenly Hosts.

Overall, my countless visions, religious dreams and spiritual experiences have taught me that Jesus will always be there for us in all circumstances in life whether we realize this or not at the time. It's also imperative for us to understand that if we ask, then we shall receive; if we seek God, we shall always find Him; if we knock on God's door, it shall be opened to us. If we turn to Jesus during our time of need, God will never reject us and He will always assist us, even when nobody else can.

God will never give up on us, even during the times that we may have given up on Him; Jesus will always welcome us back, even after we have strayed from Him. And as our Shepherd, Jesus will leave the ninety-nine sheep behind to search for the one lost sheep in particular, that has strayed from His Flock since Jesus loves every single one of us equally, and our Lord and God will always rejoice when we are found after having been lost.

Again, I would like to reiterate that we are never alone in this world since Jesus is always there with us, holding our hand, throughout both the good and bad times in our lives, just as He held my hand in my dream.

And it's of the utmost importance to always remember that if we make the effort to include God in our everyday lives and call upon His Glorious Name, then Jesus will respond by helping us in ways that our human mortal brains cannot possibly ever imagine, comprehend or understand since we are all God's Children, and are a part of God's Family. Consequently, I also know, without a doubt, that our Father, Who Art in Heaven, Hallowed Be Thy Name, as well as our Mother Mary, Queen of Heaven and of the Angels, shall always protect, look after and assist us in our daily lives, as well as love each and every one of us unconditionally, since they are our true Heavenly Parents, for all the days of our lives on this earth.

I cannot emphasize highly enough that the take-home message from this book to all of my readers who may be experiencing unspeakable and immeasurable pain and suffering worldwide is really quite simple, straightforward and black and white:

Please always remember, and never forget, that God is Hope, hope is faith, and God loves each and every one of us, unconditionally and infinitively, with all of our faults included, regardless of who we are as a person, the amount of wealth/material possessions that we may accumulate during our lifetime, our status and position in life, the sins that we have committed against God, whether or not we believe in His existence including those who have rejected God either temporarily or forever, and more than any mortal on this earth is ever capable of loving us.

In actual fact, we are indeed nothing without God, and if we place all of our faith, hope and trust in Jesus, then our dire life circumstances can dramatically change for the better in a split second, and anything is possible.

Furthermore, if we truly believe, with all of our heart, with all of our mind, with all of our soul, with all of our strength and with every living cell in our body, that nothing is impossible through God, then miracles can and will occur in our daily lives.

Personally, I have wholeheartedly responded to God's Call. I love Jesus, Our Lord and God, above all things in my life. I experience supernatural occurrences in my life on a daily basis. I have chosen to follow the path of righteousness, through my own freewill, and I live my life in accordance with the Way, the Truth and the Life. I serve God and God alone, and I shall accomplish His Will to the very best of my abilities until the day I become deceased, and pass from this life and into the next.

If you choose to become a Disciple of Jesus, through your own freewill, love God with all of your heart, mind, soul and strength, and follow the path of righteousness, then you may also become as spiritually close to Jesus and to His magnificent Archangels – Prince St Michael, St Raphael the Healer and St Gabriel Archangel, as I am today, and you may even encounter supernatural occurrences either on a daily or intermittent basis, as a result.

I strongly believe, without any semblance of doubt whatsoever, that nothing is impossible through God and that indeed, anything is possible through Jesus Christ, our Lord and God, Who is the Saviour and Light of our world.

My life is meaningless without God, and I adore Him because He never forces me to do anything against my will; Jesus loves me most unconditionally and infinitely for the person that I am and the person that I have chosen to become in life as a result of my own freewill.

My visions, religious dreams and spiritual experiences discussed in this book are proof and verification that Jesus Christ, our Lord and God, the Immaculate Virgin Mary, God's most Holy Angels, the Saints, Heaven, Hell and Satan all really do exist, and I am a living testament to this.

I am Linda Virage, and this is my story.

www.ingramcontent.com/pod-product-compliance
Lightning Source LLC
Chambersburg PA
CBHW030254010526
44107CB00053B/1701